THE

INDIAN PASS.

BY

ALFRED B. STREET,

AUTHOR OF "FUGITIVE POEMS;" "FRONTENAC," A POEM; "FOREST PICTURES IN
THE ADIRONDACKS," A SERIES OF POEMS; "THE COUNCIL OF REVISION;
WITH SKETCHES OF ITS MEMBERS AND EARLY COURTS, AND ITS
VETOES;" "WOODS AND WATERS; OR, SUMMER IN THE
SARANACS," ETC., ETC.

NEW YORK
HURD AND HOUGHTON, PUBLISHERS.
Cambridge: Riverside Press.
1869.

Reprinted by
PURPLE MOUNTAIN PRESS
Fleischmanns, New York
1993

Unabridged reprint of the 1869 edition by
PURPLE MOUNTAIN PRESS, LTD.
Main Street, PO Box E3
Fleischmanns, New York 12430-0378

1993

Library of Congress Cataloging-in-Publication Data

Street, Alfred Billings, 1811? -1881.
    The Indian Pass / Alfred B. Street.
        p.   cm.
    Originally published: New York : Hurd and Houghton, 1869.
    ISBN 0-935796-41-X (acid-free paper)
    1. Adirondack Mountains (N.Y.) 2. Essex County (N.Y.) -
-Description and travel.   I. Title.
    F127.A2S8   1993
    917.47'530441--dc20   93-19773
                                                                  CIP

Manufactured in the United States of America
Printed on acid-free paper

Dedication.

—◆—

The sympathy and kindness of three friends encouraged me to publish this record of pleasant hours passed in the mountain-forests of the State of which we are all native, and to

LYMAN TREMAIN, DANIEL B. ST. JOHN,

AND

JOHN H. REYNOLDS,

I GRATEFULLY INSCRIBE IT.

THE AUTHOR.

ALBANY, December, 1868.

CONTENTS.

CHAPTER I.

THE INDIAN PASS.

CHAPTER II.

THE INDIAN PASS.

CHAPTER III.

MOUNT MARCY.

CHAPTER IV.

MOUNT MARCY.

CHAPTER V.

WHITEFACE.

CHAPTER VI.

SUNDRIES.

CHAPTER VII.

THE GORGE OF THE DIAL.

INTRODUCTION.

THE history of Essex County (which county forms the scene of the wanderings described in the following work) comprises the history of the mountain region of Northern New York, and, as such, should be known to the people of the State of which Essex is the most remarkable and interesting portion. Organized in 1799, in the division of Clinton County, it is the second in territorial extent (St. Lawrence being the first) in the State, several of its Townships (Newcomb, Schroon, Minerva, Keene, and North Elba) being larger than some of the counties. It embraces nine tenths of the mountain system of the entire State, and the whole (except a few detached summits) of the northern portion, including as it does the five parallel ranges described in the commencement of this work. It thus bears the name of the Switzerland of the North, and is full of natural wonders and redolent of romance.

Indeed, Swiss travellers have acknowledged that
while its peaks do not attain the height of theirs, it
fully equals their country in romantic grandeur.

One thousand seven hundred and seventy-nine
square miles compose the area of this wild, mountain county. Its north is bounded by the counties
of Franklin and Clinton, with the Ausable River
forming its northeastern line ; along its eastern
border stretches Lake Champlain ; it is bounded
south by Warren County, with its extreme southeastern portion joined by the northeastern penin-
sulated point of Washington County ; and on the
west by the counties of Hamilton and Franklin.

The home of nearly the whole of the Adirondack
group (the Clinton Range, of which this group is the
heart, passing nearly centrally through the county),
of all its tallest peaks, and boasting an average height
of three thousand feet above Lake Champlain, the
county forms the great water-shed of the State north
of the Mohawk River. Its three towns of Newcomb,
North Elba, and Keene, embracing within their
limits Mounts Marcy, McIntyre, Colden, and Santanoni, compose in turn the water-shed of the county, sending, like overflowing urns, streams in every
direction, that find their way into the Atlantic —
north by the St. Lawrence, and south by the Bay
of New York.

The Clinton, or (as it is now most generally called from the group) the Adirondack Range, the most important of the five ranges, attains the greatest general elevation of any range east of the Rocky Mountains, although its loftiest crest, Mount Marcy, is exceeded by one mountain at the east and some three or four other summits at the south of the nation.

The following mountains are comprised within the limits of the county : Mount Marcy, and Haystack ; Mounts Colden and McIntyre; Wallface ; Mounts Robertson and Henderson; Santanoni; Boreas Mountain; The Dial; The Gothics, and Whiteface (the above forming, with Mount Seward in Franklin County, and Blue Mountain in Hamilton, the Adirondack group). Moose Mountain ; Mounts Baldwin, Goodenow, and Joseph ; McKenzie's Pond Mountain; the Keene Summits (with local names, among which are, Big Pitch-off at Edmunds' Ponds, The Noon-Mark, and Rogers' Mountain) ; Dix's Peak ; Macomb Mountain ; Owl's Head ; The Dome, or Giant of the Valley ; Bald Peak of North Hudson ; Bulwagga Mountain ; Bald Peak of Moriah ; Hoffman's and Schroon Mountains ; Mounts Pharaoh, Defiance, and Discovery ; Lead, Buck, and Boquet Mountains ; Split Rock ; the

Elizabethtown Peaks (The Raven, Wood-Hill, The
Cobble, and Hurricane Peak) ; Green Mountain ;
Little Pitch-off; Saddle Mountain ; Mount Lyon ;
Mount Esther ; Leggett Mountain ; Mountains of
the Jay Range (Mounts Ebenezer, Bassett, Hamlin,
Clark, and Haystack) ; Poke O'Moonshine ; Bos-
worth Mountain, and Trembleau Point.

The four or five hundred other mountains in the
county either bear obscure local names or are
unnamed.

These mountains rise (with two or three excep-
tions) from two to five thousand feet and upward
in height, none being lower than a thousand or fifteen hundred feet. They are wild and savage to
the last degree. Beautiful lakes, into which torrents
tumble, bathe their feet, and offer crystal mirrors
to their rugged features.

The native forest covers the acclivities from base
to within five hundred feet of the summit (as regards
the tallest peaks), where the gradually lessening
trees become shrubs, and the dwarf pine-tree, lying
flat, yields to the firm strong juniper, which soon
vanishes into stern cold crags, scattered over with
Alpine mosses, grasses, and varieties of Alpine
plants.

Of this forest, the evergreens or soft woods, — the

pine, hemlock, fir, spruce, and white cedar, — are found on the more ascending flanks, and near the rocky crests of the mountains ; while on the intermediate grounds, and at the foot of the slopes, are the deciduous hard wood trees, — beech, black birch, bird's-eye or sugar-maple, red and black maple, white and black ash, the red and black cherry, black-walnut, butternut, elm, and white oak ; with the deciduous soft woods, — the alder, willow, wild poplar, moose-missee, or mountain ash, white birch and tamarack.

The Adirondack group at first sight appears to be thrown together without order or system, but inspection resolves it into an irregular circle or ellipse with the longitudinal axes of the detached mountains composing the ellipse trending from the southwest to the northeast, the direction of the range in which the group is situated.

Forty years ago, this group (except to the hunter, trapper, and occasional sportsman) was unknown. In 1832, however, the State, under the administration of Governor Marcy, directed a survey to ascertain its resources, mineral, agricultural, and otherwise, which survey was continued under the succeeding administration of Governor Seward. Essex County, as a portion of the Second Geological District, fell under

b

the able supervision of Professor Ebenezer Emmons,
who particularly explored the mountain group, to
which he affixed the name of The Adirondacks, after
the Indian nation which, before their expulsion by
the Iroquois, claimed the region as a part of their
hunting-grounds. These grounds extended south of
the St. Lawrence, west of Lake Champlain, east of
the Great Lakes, and north of the Mohawk Valley.

He affixed likewise the present names to several
of the crests before unnamed, namely, Mounts
Marcy, Seward, McIntyre, Colden, Henderson, and
Dix's Peak. Scientific and literary tourists followed,
particularly Professors F. N. Benedict (who in fact
had preceded Prof. Emmons in the region) and
James Hall, with W. C. Redfield, and Dr. James
Eights, of the former, and Charles F. Hoffman and
Joel T. Headley of the latter class ; but even then
their writings described a region strange as the
steppes of Tartary.

That the Adirondack nation, and after them the
Iroquois, traversed if they did not inhabit the region,
does not admit a doubt. Tradition asserts that
the partisan Rogers, so famous for his exploits at
Lake George, destroyed, in the absence of the warriors, an Indian village on the Plains of Abraham,
in the town of North Elba. He was pursued and

overtaken by the warriors of the tribe at the Boquet River, just below Elizabethtown, where a battle
took place. Traces of Indian occupancy also occur
at other localities, in the shape of rusty knives,
hatchets, arrow-heads, and pottery.

Still these traces are slight, except at North Elba
and around the Saranac Lakes, owing probably to
the stern nature of the mountain tracts and density
of the wild forest, in comparison with the beautiful
uplands and valleys of the more open woods and
softer portions of the State. The frowning forest
south of Mount Seward and extending to the Chain
Lakes was named by the savages Coux-a-cra-ga, or
the Dismal Wilderness. It frowns now the same
as it did then. Mitchell Sabattis, the Indian guide,
informed the writer, but five years since, that the
larger portion had never been trodden by a white
man. Trappers from other points hover in winter
at its edges, snaring their game among the frozen
drifts on snowshoes, but do not penetrate its dark,
tangled, unknown recesses.

No doubt, however, exists that particular tribes
inhabited particular spots, especially the romantic
Saranac Lakes, region of purple skies and silver
waters. But to the general slight impress left upon
the region by the red man may probably be traced

the general want of Indian nomenclature. Few Indian names exist, and of such as do, some were affixed by writers according to their fancy. The following have been found by the writer. More, probably exist; while such termonology as could be obtained is appended.

Adirondack, Wood or Tree-Eaters, from the Iroquois word Ga-ron-dah, Trees, and Ha-des, meaning, They eat. Hence the Iroquois word Ha-de-ron-dack, changed by the French language into A-di-ron-dack, the *h* being dropped and the French *i* pronounced like the English *e*. An Indian nation in old times attacked the Iroquois, who drove them north around Saratoga and Lake Champlain, where they sued for peace, which was granted by the Iroquois, who taunted them by saying that they had become so weak and powerless they could not kill game but had been forced to eat trees.

Mount Marcy : Tahawus, He splits the Sky. This name was either discovered or invented by that fine poet and profound Indian scholar and antiquarian, Charles F. Hoffman (and he is accredited as authority concerning the name by Henry R. Schoolcraft). If Mr. Hoffman invented the name, both fact and name form a striking and characteristic illustration of his bold, poetic, and original genius.

Mount Seward: Ou-kor-lah, The Great Eye.

Santanoni: Si-non-do-wanne, The Great Mountain.

Mount McIntyre: He-no-ga, Home of the Thunderer.

Mount Colden: Ou-no-war-lah, Scalp Mountain. From the baring of the rock by the slides.

Bald Peak (North Hudson): O-no-ro-no-rum, Bald Head.

Whiteface: Thei-a-no-gu-en, White Head. With reference to the naked white rock at its summit. Also Wa-ho-par-te-nie.

Hurricane Peak: No-do-ne-yo, Hill of the Wind.

Mount Pharaoh: On-de-wa, Black Mountain.

Ticonderoga: Che-on-de-ro-ga, Where the Waters meet. It has eleven other Indian names.

Kayadarosseras, The Lake Country.

Indian Pass: He-no-do-aw-da, The Path of the Thunderer. Also Os-ten-wanne, Great Rock; Otne-yar-heh, The Stonish Giants; and Ga-nos-gwah, Giants clothed with stone.[1]

Whiteface Clove: Kur-loo-na, Spot of the

---

[1] See note at the end of the Introduction.

Death-song. From the murmur of the pines in the Clove.

Ausable Forks : Tei-o-ho-ho-gen, The Forks of a River.

Flume of the Opalescent River : Gwi-en-dau-qua, A Hanging Spear.

The Iron Dam at the village of the Upper Works : Tsi-nag-she, Place of Beavers.

Lake Champlain : Caniadare Guarante, The Door of the Country. Also Peta-on-bough, A Double Lake branching into two — with reference to Lake George.

Split Rock at Lake Champlain : Re-gioch-ne, or Regio Rock, or Rogeo. From the name of a Mohawk Indian drowned at the rock. It denoted the boundary between the Iroquois and St. Lawrence Indians.

Lake George : An-dia-ta-roc-ti, The Place where the Lake narrows, or where the Lake shuts itself. Also Tsi-non-drossa and Cani-deri-oit, Tail of the Lake, namely, part south of Ticonderoga. Likewise Ka-nor-do-ro, Narrows of the Lake ; and Horicon, also, Tail of the Lake, namely, appendage to Lake Champlain. Although the latter name was affixed by the great novelist Cooper, taken from an Indian tribe, yet for its beauty, euphony, and adaptation, it should be adopted as the sole name.

Lake Henderson: Ga-nu-da-yu, Handsome Lake.

Lake Colden : Ta-wis-ta-a, The Mountain Cup.

Avalanche Lake : Ta-ne-o-da-eh, Lofty Lake, or Lake high up. (Lies 2,900 feet above tide, and is considered the highest body of water in the State.)

Pharaoh Lake : On-nis-ske, White or Silver Lake.

Ausable Ponds : Ga-wis-da-ga-o, Two Goblets side by side.

Schroon Lake : Sca-ni-a-dar-oon, A large Lake. Abbreviated to Scaroon ; hence Schroon. The above is a Mohawk word found in old land papers applied to Schroon Lake. S signifies *a*, and Caniadare means lake ; oon means large. In addition : Ska-ne-ta-no-wa-na, The largest Lake. Also, Scarona, the name of an Indian girl who leaped over a precipice from her French lover, and was drowned. Likewise Rogh-qua-non-da-go, Child of the Mountain.

Schroon River : Gain-bou-a-gwe, Crooked River.

Hudson River : Co-ha-ta-te-a (Mohawk), Great River having Mountains beyond the (Cahoh) Cohoes Falls.

Also Shatemuc (Mohegan). From Shata, A Pelican or Swan. The reason of the name is unknown.

In addition, Mohegan-ittuck, Mohegan River. So called by the Minisi (a branch of the Lenni Lenape or Delawares proper), inhabiting the west banks of the River.

Likewise San-a-ta-ty : an Iroquois word descriptive of its windings.

Farther as to the termonology : — Mount Marcy derives its name from William L. Marcy; Mount Seward, from William H. Seward; Dix's Peak, from John A. Dix ; Mount McIntyre, from Archibald McIntyre; Mount Henderson, from David Henderson; Mount Robertson, from Archibald Robertson. Mount Colden : this mountain was formerly called Mount McMartin, from Duncan McMartin, but subsequently named after David C. Colden. (These five gentlemen were engaged in the development of the iron interest at the Upper Works.) Wallface derives from the wall of the Indian Pass ; Whiteface, from the white feldspar at its summit, bared by a slide ; The Noon-Mark, from the sun standing over its top at noon ; Big Pitch-off, from a leaning rock of five hundred feet at the northeast corner of its crest ; Little

Pitch-off, from its impending appearance ; and both also from Pitch of mountain : The Gothics, from their dark, wild aspect ; Schroon Lake : in addition to the four Indian names, accounts state the lake was named by French officers from Crown Point Scarron (hence Schroon) Lake, in honor of Madame Scarron, afterward Madame de Maintenon. (By this name — Scaron — it is also called on Governor Tryon's map of 1779, and likewise on the map of 1796.) The Raven derives from such a bird shot upon the mountain by the first explorer for the State Road from Sandy Hill to the Canada line. Wood Hill, from its leafy look ; The Cobble, generally supposed to be from the rock resting on its summit, but more evidently from its want of being cobbled or mended, or, as the phrase now goes, "reconstructed ; " Hurricane Peak, from a lurking wind rushing at all that climb the ascent ; Boquet River, named by William Gilliland, from the flowers upon its banks. Some assert it derives its name from Colonel Boquet, who encamped upon its borders, but it bore the name before his appearance. Others derive it from Baquet, the French for bucket ; others again from Bosquet, a thicket. Willsborough, from William Gilliland its founder ; Elizabethtown, from the wife of Mr. Gilliland ; Saddle Mountain, from its hollowed summit; Santanoni, changed probably from the Indian word Si-non-do-wanne, or as it is generally asserted, a corruption of St. Anthony; Poke O'Moonshine comes from its dark "pokerish" aspect; and Trembleau Point from Trompe a l'eau Point, the French for Tongue in the Water.

The county having, as observed, an average height of three thousand feet above tide, it is interesting to note the following table of heights above tide water: —

Lake Champlain, 93 feet; Mount McIntyre, 5,183; Wallface, 2,000; Mount Henderson, 3,000; Santanoni, 5,000; Whiteface, 5,000; Colden, 5,000; The Dial, 4,900; Boreas Mountain, 3,726; Dix's Peak, 5,200; Mount Pharaoh, 4,000; Schroon Mountain, 3,200; Poke O'Moonshine, 3,000; Bosworth Mountain, 3,000; Mount Goodenow, and Moose Mountain, 3,000; Hurricane Peak, 3,000; The Raven, 2,000; Mount Discovery, 2,000; Mounts Hamlin, Clark, and Bassett, each 2,000; Owl's Head, 2,706; Lake Avalanche, 2,900; Lake Colden, 2,851; Lake Henderson, 1,936; Lake Sanford, 1,826; Preston Ponds, 1,700; Village of the Upper Works, 1,889; Mountain Meadow, on side of Mount Marcy, source of the Opalescent, or northeast branch of the Hudson, 4,747; INDIAN PASS, 2,817 (from its base); MOUNT MARCY, 5,467.

The whole fall of the Adirondack River, from its source in the Indian Pass, five miles, to the Upper Works, is 1,130 feet; thence to tide, 2,109 feet; aggregate fall, 3,239 feet.

Snow remains on Mount Marcy until the middle of July, and ice forms every night throughout the summer, while in the Indian Pass, and Gorge of the Dial the ice does not melt throughout the year.

The Valleys are, the Keene and Ausable Valley (considered as one), the Valley of North Elba, or the Plains of Abraham, the elevated valley or plateau of Alsted's Hill, the valleys of the Upper Hudson waters, and the beautiful Valley of the Boquet, comprising most of the arable land of the county.

Into these valleys, composed of a warm, rich, sandy loam, and very fertile, rural life has entered, turning the wilderness into grain-field and meadow, where the kine graze, the flocks nibble, and the tawny Harvest reaps his priceless treasures. Here stands the farm-house with its barn, well-sweep, or spring, and slanting orchard trees. Cultivation leaves every year his wandering, rough foot-prints on the lower mountain slopes and amid the bordering woods, in stony lot or stumpy clearing, with

his log-hut by purling stream or dashing fall. But
the general area of the county is little improved,
buried in the forest that has only seen the hatchet
of the hunter flashing in the erection of the bush
shanty, his form pictured in the pure waters while
searching for the trout, or glancing among the trees
rousing the deer. The deepest wilds remain as
when " the morning stars sang together," where
the sprout rises to the tree, which, falling into the
trunk, mingles amid its moss with its original elements, and no human eye to mark the changes.

But softness and beauty are not wanting. Wild
meadows or " parks " occur at intervals, grouped
in thickets and sprinkled with trees like cultivated
lawns ; old beaver meadows are found deep in the
beaver grass, and edged with saplings sawn asunder by the beaver's tooth with the little pond
blinking to the hawk wheeling around the bordering pine-tree, and with the rill singing through to
the white-weed and blue-grass ; glades are encountered, green in the wild glade-grass and spangled
with the white clover ; dells smile, fit haunt for
fairies, where the thrasher pipes, the scampering
squirrel barks, and the gliding rabbit jerks its long
ears at every sound ; and the ancient path of the
whirlwind is seen with the wrenched trees long

since melted into the grass of a vista like an old settler-road, so that the eye looks in vain for the faint wheel track.

An interesting marvel attends the forest. Evergreens, swept by fire or the axe, are followed by deciduous trees. Where the strong pine dared the storm, the light poplar trembles ; and where the dark hemlock frowned, the white-birch glitters.

Next among these appear the hardier trees. The beech shines in its vernal satin where the rough spruce hung its scaly cones ; and where the dull fir-tree curved, the maple shows its globe of autumn crimson.

Here roam the panther, the great black bear, the wolf, the wild-cat, the beautiful deer, the infrequent moose, lynx, and wolverine ; the fisher, sable, otter, mink, muskrat, pine-marten, fox, badger, woodchuck rabbit, and the varieties of the squirrel.

Among the birds are the grand black war eagle ; the species of the hawk, owl, loon, and duck ; the crane, heron, raven, crow, stake-driver, mud-hen, brown thrasher (Saranac nightingale), the partridge, blue jay, blackbird, kingfisher, and mountain finch. The robin of the orchard, the wren of the garden, the bobolink of the pasture field, and the red and tawny oriole of the meadow-elm haunt the hamlet and clearing at the forest's edge.

Among the insects are the silver chirping wood
cricket, whose little lute yields magic to the night;
the fire-fly, the fairy will-o'-the-wisp of the lake and
stream ; the gemmed dragon-fly, the flashing arrow
of the water-blossoms; the gold-tinted deer-fly, the
wandering spangle of the shallow grasses; the water-
spider, that jerks furrowing over the liquid crystal ;
and (horrible memory!) the Satanically beautiful
black fly, the ever thirsty and never daunted; the
fearful mosquito, whose bagpipe precedes his dart,
as the song of the rattlesnake his fang; and the
villainous midge, sparks of fire upon the skin.

Lake shad and pickerel are found in Lake Champlain; the salmon, with its rich yellow flesh, in Lake
George ; the salmon trout, and (in the spring
months and in June) the speckled trout, in all the
lower forest lakes ; while throughout the rest of
the season, the latter swarm in the pure swift
spring brooks; and the outlets and inlets of the
diamond-clear expanses.

In the lakes and streams of the upper region,
however, no trout are found, while below the
mountain torrents they are plentiful. Lakes Sanford and Henderson abound with them, but the
lofty Avalanche Lake harbors only a small lizard.

The Flora of Essex is richer than that of any

other county in the State, and rewards more the search of the botanist in the rare specimens it affords.

Among the most beautiful of the flowering plants, may be mentioned the species of clematis, virgin bower, one of which climbing on trees and shrubs mingles its clusters of large purple flowers with the green foliage of the supporting branches. In the valleys and about the lakes and ponds, many species of the orchis family find a home. Of these curious plants some of the finest are the *Arethusa bulbosa,* (bulbous arethusa) ; the *Pogonia ophioglossoides ;* the *Calapogon,* or grass-pink, and the *Orchis spectabilis.*

Seven or eight species of viola are found in this region, and plants and shrubs of the rose tribe abound. On the summits of the highest mountains are many rare plants, some of them only found elsewhere in extreme northern latitudes. The *Arenaria groenlandica* (Greenland sandroot), and *Potentilla tridentata* (white cinquefoil), are only found on the loftiest peaks of these mountains, or of the White Mountains, New Hampshire, while the golden-rod of Whiteface and Mount Marcy are found on no other mountains in the State.

There are two beautiful specimens of kalmia or

laurel found in the marshes; also two exquisite
species of azalea, a pink and a white, seen in
marshes and on shady hill-sides; and in the meadows
a very beautiful species of *Iris ochroleuca* (yellow
iris,) a large splendid yellow flower growing in the
town of Lewis.[1]

The surface of the county glitters a net-work of
lakes, ponds, and streams. The first two lie in long
and narrow clefts of the hypersthene rock, with an
extent ranging from a few acres to twenty miles.
Steep, densely wooded mountains soar from their
sides, yielding a dark gloss to the molten silver of
these lovely chalices; fairy bays indent their borders,
and leafy points jut out; spring brooks tinkle in;
outlets, bowers of branches, creep forth; while the
amber shallows are fringed with water-grasses tufted
by purple mooseheads, red Mohawk tassels, and
tawny flags that gleam with flying insects, and glow
in mosaics of silver and gold from the white and
yellow water-lilies.

These expanses fall into three systems: the system of Whiteface (north), that of Mount Marcy
(centre), and of Mount Pharaoh (south). Among

[1] Found by Dr. George T. Stevens, of Albany, N. Y. No other
botanist has met with it in the limits of this State. Several other
species have been found by him in this county which have never been
reported as native of the State.

the two or three hundred of these expanses are portions of Lakes Champlain, George, and Schroon ; Lakes Placid and Henderson (with Lake Harkness) ; Lake Sanford (with Lakes Jamie and Sallie) ; Lakes Colden, Avalanche, Moose, Newcomb, Delia, Rich, Harris ; several of the Chain Lakes, with Pharaoh and Paradox Lakes.

The Ponds are, Mackenzie's, the three Preston Ponds, the three ponds of Wallface ; Moose, Bennett's, Connery, Copperas, Owen's, Oliver's, Round, Whortleberry, Crane, Lizard, Puts, Long (of Schroon), Long (of Elizabethtown), Crookneck, Pyramid, Johnson's, Bartlett, Ensign's, Crowfoot, Bullpout, New, Black, Spring, Two Story, the two Edmunds', the two Ausable, Rattlesnake, Warm, Butternut, and Auger Ponds. The rest are principally unnamed.

This labyrinth or net-work of water is in turn intertwined with rivers, creeks, streams, and rills, forming a water system most curious for its intricacy. Two gorges, the Indian Pass and the Gorge of the Dial, give birth to three rivers, the Hudson, the Ausable, and the Boquet, which after nearly interlocking their fountains (the first two quite), flow to entirely different points of the compass. The main stream of the Ausable's west branch

c

(called the Notch stream) flows from the north-east portal of the Indian Pass, and the Adirondack or main stream of the Hudson, from the southwest. From the north opening of the Dial gorge flows the south branch of the Boquet, and from the south opening, the west branch of the Schroon River, which river forms the east branch of the Hudson.

The springs of the Ausable and Hudson in the centre of the Indian Pass rise so close to each other (in freshets they actually mingle), that the wild-cat lapping the water of the one may bathe his rear feet in the other, and the rock rolling from the precipice could scatter spray from both in the same concussion.

In addition to the three rivers are the greater portion of Rock River, from the Chain Lakes, emptying into the Hudson, and the last portion of Indian River running into the same stream; the Opalescent emptying into Lake Sanford; Boreas River, with its east, middle, and west branches, flowing likewise into the Hudson; Putnam's Creek, Mill Brook, and Ti Creek emptying into Lake Champlain; Trout and Roaring Brooks, Black Creek and The Branch flowing into the Boquet; and Chubb River into the Ausable.

Our noble river, the Hudson, draws birth from

this county, and a truly magnificent birth is it. Its three main cradles are the Indian Pass, the towering meadow of Tahawus, and the Gorge of the Dial. It flows from the Pass into Lakes Henderson and Sanford as the Adirondack River ; thence downward as the Hudson, it receives the Boreas River and enters the County of Warren.

Its east branch, the Schroon, issuing from New Pond and the Dial Gorge, flows into Schroon Lake, the lower half of which extends into Warren County.

The branches of these two streams find source or are connected, in this county alone, with a score of lakes, among which (beside Henderson and Sanford) are Lakes Colden, Avalanche, Newcomb, Delia, Rich, Harris, several of the Chain Lakes, Schroon Lake as to its upper half, and Paradox Lake : and as many ponds ; — linking thus many a grand mountain, and threading leagues on leagues of deepest forest, yielding home and drink to myriads of wild animals and birds. Down into Warren County it goes, welcoming the Schroon, with many another stream, and reaching its hands to many a far-away lake, including the one on the Crane Mountain crest, — eye of the rocky face the mountain lifts toward the cloud ; down, still down

it moves, uniting the Sacondaga with its east and
west branches from Piseco Lake and Lake Pleasant, and clasping many a brook with the outlets
of many a broad water. Saratoga Lake sends its
creek, to swell the flood ; the Batten Kill and the
Hoosick flow into it; then comes the Mohawk, with
its East and West Canada Creeks from the north,
clustered with their own system of streams and
ponds; and Schoharie Creek from the south; thence
widening and deepening it sweeps still downward
until through its two stately bays it reaches the
ocean.

The bubble that bursts under the wall of the
Indian Pass, disdains a lowlier grave than the Atlantic wall between the Old World and the New.

Wild as are the river's upward ways, its wildest
way is toward the Racket waters. Upward it
reaches its northwest finger, up, up, beyond the
deserted clearing and sunken cabin of the settler ;
beyond the log shanty of the hunter, and the leafy
shed of the trapper ; beyond the rifle-shot at the
deer, and the dropped angle for the trout ; beyond
even the lurking trap for the fisher and sable ; up
to where the panther's print lies fresh, and the
wolf's red eye-ball only spots the night gloom of
the woods. Up winds the stream, — a rivulet, a

streak, a glitter, a glint, — vanishing at last into a tuft of dripping moss. Thus the west branch of the grand river is traced to Hendrick Spring, within a mile east of Long Lake, an expansion of the Racket River. The crimson cluster of the mountain-ash, where the fawn day by day draws its drink, with never a human step to daunt it, scarce finds room to dip in the same water that floated the Great Eastern beside the crowds of the nation's metropolitan city. Truly a great king is the Hudson, bearing to immortality the name of its discoverer. Truly, rather, a stately Indian Sachem with his lofty brow of leafy plumes and his four Indian names, stalking down from his wild mountains among his meeting vassals, until, doffing his forest mantle sprinkled with jewels for one woven of meadow-grass and grainfield, with lace-work edge of roof and steeple, and discarding his sceptre of cedar for one compacted of wild-flowers and garden roses, he treads his smooth way, — a civilized monarch,— to kneel at last at the foot of his Emperor the sea.

To regard our noble and diversified River under another aspect : He is the well-dressed cit driving his gleaming wheels between his freestone fronts ; or toiling amid his busy warehouses fringed with

masts, while all around glide steamboats and rail-
cars, and flash telegraph wires; he is the rustic vil-
lager lounging with his hands in his pockets along
sleepy houses, or hanging around corners waiting for
the daily post-coach; he is the brown-hued farmer
on green hill-sides and in smiling valleys, scattering
the seed, guiding the plough, or handling scythe and
pitchfork; he is the rough backwoodsman wielding
the axe among the trees, and rearing the log-cabin
in the bushy clearing; he is the wild hunter on
the mountain-slopes and in the rocky gorges kneeling in ambush for the game, and crouching to taste
the chalice of the brook; he is the wilder trapper
fixing his wooden deadfall by the leafy stream or
hiding his steel-trap in the bushes of the blazed
trees; he (changing his nature) is the loon shout-
ing on the distant lake; the deer browsing on the
lily-pads of the grassy shallow; the catamount peal-
ing his hungry cry where the cascade dashes among
the dwindling trees; the eagle pluming his wing on
the blasted pine where the craggy torrent leaps;
the moose feeding on the tap-borers of the rushy
water in the far-away wild meadow; the beaver
plastering his infrequent dome in the lurking pond;
and lastly, the speckled trout prowling in the pool,
scores of feet only from the silver globule swelling
from the crevice.

The scenery of Essex is that of the primitive formation — gorges, ravines, and steep ascents — combining in the highest degree beauty with grandeur. Its line of shore along Lake Champlain forms the noblest scenery of the lake ; its valleys are full of rural loveliness ; its mountains and gorges are sublime to terror ; its rivers pure and picturesque, while from every peak stretch views of surpassing splendor. From the acclivity between Port Kent and Keeseville, the water-scapes of Lake Champlain are peerless in their beauty, changing like a panorama with the turnings of the road ; while at every hand are presented mountains, woods, and waters, shining in the loveliest tints, and which will form, when known, the paradise of art.

Natural curiosities abound throughout the county. That others are buried in the terrific forests still darkening two thirds of the surface, cannot be doubted.

Among the curiosities known are Lake Paradox, whose outlet in high water flows back on the lake ; the pond on the summit of Mount Joseph, whose rim is close upon the edge ; the mingling of the fountains of the Hudson and Ausable in freshets in the Indian Pass ; the torrent dashes or lace-work from the greater or lesser rain down the grooved side of

Mount Colden toward Lake Avalanche; the three lakes on the top of Wallface, sending streams into the St. Lawrence by Cold River and the Racket, into Lake Champlain by the Ausable, and the Atlantic by the Hudson; the enormous rocks of the Indian Pass standing upon sharp edges on steep slopes, and looking as if the deer breaking off against them his yearly antlers would topple them headlong, yet defying unmoved the mighty agencies of frost, and plumed with towering trees; with all the cavern intricacy between and underneath the fallen masses, where the ice gleams unmelted throughout the year; and the same rock intricacy in the Panther Gorge of Mount Marcy.

The throbbing of the water of Lake Placid into a neighboring pond (Paradox Pond) through a connecting stream (with no other outlet or inlet), and the responsive throb of the pond's back-water into the lake, is an interesting fact, vouched by eye-witnesses.[1]

In addition are the two subterranean passages in Schroon, near Paradox Lake; one the channel of a stream, the other a Gothic arch through which a large stream likewise dashes.

[1] See Winslow C. Watson's admirable description of Essex County, in the State Agricultural Transactions of 1853. The writer was informed of the same circumstance by Robert G. Scott of North Elba.

The Port Kendall chasm, also, through which a brook bounds in a fall of two score feet into Lake Champlain; and Split Rock cloven into a wall of thirty feet from a promontory of the Lake, and forming a watery passage of ten feet between; and lastly, the greatest of all its natural curiosities, — the INDIAN PASS and MOUNT MARCY.

The Geological formation of the county opens a field unequaled in the State. Here is the exclusive home of the hypersthene rock, or rather the mass composed of Labrador feldspar and hypersthene, mostly of the former, but bearing the specific name of the latter. This primary gray, iron-bearing rock extends in a triangular shape through the county, forming the basis rock and a large proportion of the surface (and in some the whole surface) of eleven towns, namely, Schroon, Moriah, Keene, Elizabethtown, Westport, Chesterfield, Wilmington, Lewis, Jay, Willsborough, and Newcomb.

To define more specifically its boundaries. Its northern limit is formed by Trembleau Point on Lake Champlain, in the neighborhood of Port Kent; thence its eastern line runs a little west of south through the western portion of the town of Essex, and midway between Westport and Elizabethtown, through Moriah and west corner of Schroon; run-

ning on through the town of Minerva, the northeast corner of the adjoining County of Hamilton,
and southeast corner of Franklin County and re-
entering Essex, it passes northeast through the town
of Wilmington returning east to Trembleau Point.

This rock, in its jointed and wedge-shaped blocks,
has been uplifted (broken from a far larger mass
underneath the earth) by the grand forces of nature, into the sharp cones and saw-like ridges of the
Adirondack group trenching on the limits of eternal
frost. It is traversed in a general east and west
course by trap dikes, and although in popular belief
it is volcanic, no traces of a crater, nor any distinct
volcanic signs (except in these dikes), are found in
the group. Among its minerals are the opalescent
feldspar, garnet, mica, and (very generally diffused)
magnetic oxide of iron.

These trap dikes seam the county in every direction, from half an inch to eighty feet in width;
the compound mass, formed of hornblende, pyroxene,
and feldspar, or sienite (hornblende and feldspar),
or pyroxene and feldspar, which composes them
being an injection into the natural fissures of the
primary rocks. Although frequent in all parts of
the county, these dikes are most numerous at Port
Henry, Split Rock, and Trembleau Point. Opened

as they sometimes are by the wedge of the frost, the scoop of the slide, or the pickaxe of some mining stream, they unfold the secrets of the rock they cut into as to the minerals and gems hidden in its stern bosom. They tell of the lurking iron, the dull lead, the flashing blood-red mica, the brown tourmalin, the gray zircon, the rosy spinelle, the green hornblende, the flesh-hued feldspar, the shining rich green coccolite, the golden jasper, the red of the garnet, and purple of the amethyst.

The deep chasm cloven by a stream within the terrific mural front of Mount Colden arching toward Avalanche Lake, shows the finest known specimen of this stony veined mass, distinguished as the Great Trap Dike. On the opposite flank of Mount McIntyre are seen the parallel fissures, from the base to the summit, of another dike; but wanting the cleavage of water, it has not been laid open.

There is also a green-stone dike on the Keene summit at Edmunds' Ponds in Keene.

The other primaries of Essex are granite, limestone, and serpentine of the unstratified, gneiss and hornblende of the stratified, and porphyry and magnetic oxide of iron of the subordinate rock.

Granite, the oldest and deepest of all the rocks, is found in the county only in limited patches, and

insulated beds.   It is seen in the town of Minerva,
in several cliffs in the south part of Elizabethtown,
and in a high cliff resting on primary limestone in
Chesterfield.   While gneiss forms some of the
loftiest ranges, granite is found but in moderate
ascents.

It is metalliferous but in a small degree, containing sulphate of copper with sulphuret of iron in
limited quantities.   It also contains crystals of feldspar, pyroxene, scapolite, and green and red tourmalin.

Limestone is an important rock in the western
portion of Essex.   It enters the county from Warren County into the town of Ticonderoga; but its
most important belt mingled with serpentine in the
larger masses, is traced in Schroon, although not in
a continuous form (in fact none of the belts are perfectly continuous), along Paradox Lake, northeasterly and about eighty rods wide, through to Port
Henry on Lake Champlain.   Insulated beds of this
igneous rock occur at Newcomb Lake (in an impure
state, however, being a mixture of coccolite and
quartz), and, dissociated from serpentine, largely
near Moriah Corners.   At Edmunds' Ponds, the
primitive limestone has been bared by a slide on
the Keene summit on the southwest side of the

ponds. It lies in the upper part of the slide in a vein from twenty to forty feet in width. In Chesterfield, near the village of Clintonville, the primary limestone is found associated with granite.

The limestone contains pyroxene in crystals, feldspar, rose-quartz, asbestus, the red mica, calcareous spar, zircon, graphite, yellow chondrodite, yellow, brown, and green tourmalin, pink spinelle, hornblende, and scapolite.

Serpentine is found in the towns of Lewis and Moriah. It is frequently associated with the primitive limestone and specular oxide of iron. When not blended, it is found in large irregular masses divided into angular blocks; not in veins or dikes, neither following a range nor composed in layers. When it accompanies the limestone it is translucent and compact, and shaly when found with the oxide of iron.

It is a beautiful rock, finely mottled and striped, and most commonly of a green color, although occasionally red, brown, or yellow, and veined with variegated hues. It contains galena and asbestus, the latter largely.

Hornblende and gneiss form (with the exception of the primary limestone and transition rocks) the whole southeastern, and a large proportion of the east part of the county.

This compound rock runs in easterly ranges up
from Warren County at the south, the first of which
ranges sparkles in Bulwagga Mountain (which it
entirely forms), on the line between the towns of
Crown Point and Moriah.   The next range terminates in a precipice of sixty feet at Lake Champlain,
a little below Port Henry.   The third, a belt nine
miles wide, after forming Bald Peak, near Lake
Champlain, terminates in its northeastern course
at the lake in high steep rocks, the main or middle branch of the range ending at Split Rock.

A line drawn from near Willsborough Falls
through the towns of Westport and Moriah to
Minerva, then northwest to the foot of Long Lake,
in Hamilton County, then, in Essex again, northeast through St. Aimand to Clinton County, would
define the locality of gneiss in Essex : all outside
the line being that rock ; inside, hypersthene.

It contains in its dissociate state but few interesting minerals.   Still tourmalin, garnet, zircon, brown
peroxide of iron, graphite, sulphuret of iron, quartz,
epidote, and pyroxene are found.

Gneiss and primary limestone are found along the
eastern border of the hypersthene in Ticonderoga,
and east part of Schroon, Moriah, and Westport,
and west portion of the town of Essex, skirting also

the west and northwest flanks of the hypersthene, and occuring largely near Newcomb Lake.

Porphyry is not frequent in Essex County. Cannon's Point, a mile or two below the village of Essex, furnishes the best specimen of this volcanic rock. It is found between layers of slate; and it is seen rearing its low columnated cliffs along the lake shore in the neighborhood of the village; in the fields, in low cliffs, and in a bluff two hundred feet in height, at a locality called Rattlesnake Den. Toward Split Rock, the lake shore is strewed with fragments of this rock.

It is spread over the surface, not like the other volcanic matter, trap, disposed in veins; and it is sprinkled with crystals of red feldspar, of which substance it is formed.

The magnetic oxide of iron is diffused throughout the county. Its ledges with their projecting lodes are found under local names (Penfield and Saxe Ore Beds, Crag Harbor, Walton, Sanford, — near Port Henry, — Barnum, Hall, and Everest's veins) in the towns of Schroon, Moriah, Crown Point, Elizabethtown, Keene, and Westport. In the town of Newcomb it occurs in a far greater degree than all the rest, particularly at and around Lakes Henderson and Sanford.

The ores found here are all of a magnetic charac-
acter ; are black in the mass, and are generally
mixtures of the protoxide and peroxide, one atom of
the former to two of the latter. They are arranged
under the names of the localities where the mines
are situated. The first noticed is the Sanford Ore,
the mine lying on the west flank of a mountain of
seven hundred feet sloping gradually to the east
border of the lake of that name, and two miles
from the village of the Upper Works.

The length of the Sanford vein is between two
and three miles. There is a vein called the Coarse-
grained Black Ore close to the Upper Works,
several houses in fact resting upon it. It is coarser
than the Sanford vein, and is computed to extend
three thousand one hundred and sixty feet, with a
width of between seven and eight hundred feet.

Another vein, called the Fine-grained Ore, lies
about eighty rods east of the site of the Works, on
a ridge overlooking the village. It extends northwest more than half a mile from the Works, or
rather the length is five thousand seven hundred
and forty-two feet, with a breadth of over one hundred and fifty feet.

On the west border of Lake Henderson, nearly a
mile from the village, is another vein of fine-grained

ore ; another (an extensive one) on the west bank of Lake Sanford, nearly opposite the ore bed ; and still another (and from indications an abundant one) on the east side of the Sanford Mountain. In fact, there is reason to believe that the magnetic oxide underlies the whole valley of the Adirondack or Indian Pass River.

On the Opalescent or East River it is seen in large masses of pure ore, and on the west side of Lake Sanford, about three miles southwest from the Upper Works, is an extensive mass called (from its discoverer) the Cheney Ore Bed. Although extensive, it is not considered as valuable as the other beds, from its distance from the village and inferior quality of the ore compared with other more accessible ores.

The foreign minerals in the Sanford vein are labradorite, hypersthene, common feldspar and the crystalline green variety and hornblende.

The unaltered sedimentary rocks of Essex occupy but an extremely narrow belt along Lake Champlain.

The Potsdam Sandstone (the lowest of these rocks) is found principally at Keeseville, cloven into the chasms through which the dark Ausable plunges, and is called " The Walled Banks." The

d

southern limit of this rock in mass is the town of Willsborough; although it is seen at Ticonderoga, at the Falls and outlet of Lake George; at Mount Defiance; at Ticonderoga village; and shows itself along the shore toward Crown Point. It is seen near Bulwagga Mountain in a belt a mile wide; at Cedar Point; at Port Henry, and at Westport.

The Chazy Limestone is found near the village of Westport and in the neighborhood of the village of Essex, here, in the form of a bluff one hundred and fifty or two hundred feet above the lake.

The Trenton Limestone is found also at the village of Essex, filled with fossils, and likewise about two miles south of the same.

The Utica Slate appears at Split Rock and also a mile along the lake shore in contact with the Chazy Limestone, at which points it is traversed with trap dikes and veins of calcareous spar. It is again seen a little north of Essex, its low banks with the upper surface only exposed, traversing the shore to Peru Bay. It is confined to Essex and a few miles of the lake shore north, and in it no important minerals are found.

The Tertiary of Essex lines in insulated beds the shore of Lake Champlain, throughout the entire length of the county.

Among the minerals of the county (to recapitu-
late in some measure) are labradorite, magnetic
oxide of iron, quartz, pyroxene, feldspar, hornblende,
serpentine with carbonate of lime, graphite, asbestus, scapolite, mica, garnet, tabular spar, chondrodite, spinelle, tourmalin, zircon, idocrase, sphene,
phosphate of lime, sulphuret of iron, copper, silver,
porcelain clay and soap-stone. There is also a
mineral spring at the base of the Indian Pass.

The resources of the county are immense, and
almost entirely undeveloped. Of those geologic,
hypersthene and gneiss are the most important, not
so much in themselves as what they contain. For
ornamental purposes (tables, mantel-pieces, etc.),
the former with its rich lustre and hues, when
brought out by polishing, would prove very valuable, and furnish a fine substitute for marble. But
as the cradle of the magnetic iron ore, these ·two
rocks lift Essex County into the first rank in the
world as a wealth-producing region. The black,
heavy, magnetic block found under the hoof of
the kine in the village of the Upper Works, in
the channel of the Upper Hudson, with the water
pouring over it, fringed · by the creeping pine
at Lake Colden, trodden by the panther on the
wild banks of Avalanche Lake, and lying in its

coarse dullness beside the glittering feldspar of the
Opalescent that kindles the liquid diamond of the
mountain torrent into

> " The peacock's neck in hue,"

is the " toad " —

> " Which bears a precious jewel in its head."

The writer has picked it up in the wild meadow
of Calamity Pond, at the base of the Henderson
monument, under the shadow of the savage McIntyre, and as he looked at the shining facets of the
block, he has thought of the oriental fables of the
Genius of the Lamp, and the Magic Garden being
turned into reality by this mineral. The Genius of
the Mountain Wilderness now holds the unlighted
Lamp, but Enterprise will one day illume it, and the
splendor of the flame will dim the jeweled trees of
the Garden. One hill alone, in the southeastern part
of the town of Newcomb, is twenty feet high, and
covers forty acres. It is supposed to consist of one
solid mass of iron ore with only a slight surface of
drift.

The serpentine marble (serpentine and carbonate
of lime), in its varieties from deep to pale-green, is
a source of wealth. It receives a fine, although
not a perfect polish, from the softer serpentine wearing down more rapidly than the lime, unless great

care and fine materials are used in first smoothing the surface. The dark-green, light-veined variety is considered equal to the Italian, and superior, from its delicacy, to the Egyptian marble.

In addition is the graphite, or black lead for pencils, and porcelain clay (from the disintegration of both hypersthene and granite) for fire-brick.

Silver also without doubt exists, although its locality is for the present lost.

The county's agricultural products are Indian wheat, rye, wheat, barley, buckwheat, potatoes, carrots, beets, turnips, large crops of corn and oats, yellow and white clover, red-top, blue-joint, timothy, apples, wild plums, the wild or thorn-apple, wild grapes, and groves of wild cherries.

The soil, as shown by its trees, is of the most diversified character. Here the sycamore waves its wide branches betraying the alluvial formation; there the luxuriant butternut proclaims the rich limestone, in contrast to the dwarf oak and yellow pine of the arid plain, and the chestnut of the lean, magnesian slate.

Added to the more obvious treasures of the forest in the shape of masts and spars, timber for all purposes, and cord-wood, the grained woods of oak, birch, and maple form immense means of wealth.

The surfaces of these splendid woods when polished possess a value and show a beauty rivaling the tropical rose-wood and mahogany. The rich knots and silken shadings of the oak, the mottled surface of the birch, and above all the veiny windings of the curled maple and speckled satin of the bird's-eye, form American fabrics which should glitter in the dwellings of the American nation.

The historical annals of Essex County are full of interest. In May, 1609, Champlain discovered the lake which bears his name, and near Ticonderoga occurred the battle between him at the head of his soldiers and Algonquin allies, and the confederated Iroquois, in which the latter were defeated, and where the foundation of the hatred which those warlike savages ever after bore the French was laid.

Champlain, as the representative of the French monarch, took possession of the whole region as French territory.

The bold bluff of Ticonderoga soon arrested the military eye of France, and in 1706 a fortress was there erected, commanding the narrow straits of Lake Champlain at that point. Marquis du Quesne was the projector of the fortress, but it was built by his successor, in whose honor it was called Fort Vaudreuil. Its other French name was

Fort Carillon, "a chime of bells," with reference to the chiming of the rapid Lake George outlet at its junction with the lake.

Twenty-five years after, or in 1731, Crown Point was taken possession of by the French, and Fort St. Frederick (named after Frederick Maurepas, Secretary of State to the then reigning monarch Louis XV.) built. Previous to this, however, French settlers occupied both sides of the lake. Six years subsequently the Sieur Robert, the royal store-keeper at Montreal, obtained a seigniory embracing all the present town of Essex and the greater part of Willsborough. In 1755 the expedition of Sir William Johnson occurred, which eventuated in the battle of Lake George (three battles in one day), fought by him and Gen. Lyman against the French troops and Indians commanded by Baron Dieskau, in which Sir William was victorious, and the subsequent building by the victor of Fort William Henry on the battle-ground, and named after the Duke of Cumberland, brother to George the Second, the reigning monarch. The succeeding year witnessed the partisan exploits of Stark and Rogers around Putnam's Creek. About this time Israel Putnam became an actor in the warlike scenes of the county, the creek receiving its name from the daring warrior. The year following saw the white plume of Montcalm glancing over the silver of Lake George from Lake Champlain toward Fort William Henry for its reduction; but the fierce red of his savage allies' war-paint was not redder than the hue that steeped that plume after the surrender of the fort by its commander, Colonel Monroe. Not the warlike tomb hollowed for his ashes before Quebec by the exploding shell, two years thereafter, shields his memory from the stern reproach of history.

In 1758 a seigniory was likewise granted to Monsieur d'Alainville, of Ticonderoga, Crown Point, and Schroon.

In this year happened the expedition of Lord Howe and Sir William Johnson against Ticonderoga (the point at which England aimed her constant efforts) in Abercrombie's campaign, which kindled Lake George with its romantic and warlike array, resulting in the death of the gallant young nobleman.

In 1759 occurred the campaign of General Amherst, leading the seventh English army (and the last which passed through Lake George) against Ticonderoga; and in July of that year the French power was broken on Lake Champlain, in the surrender of Fort Carillon (Ticonderoga) by Colonel Bourlemaque, its commander, to General Amherst, who took possession in August of Fort St. Frederick, and in its place partially built the fort of Crown Point, which was never completed. In 1780 General Haviland led an army from Crown Point to Montreal, and uniting with Generals Amherst and Murray, forced in September the capitulation of Governor Vaudreuil, and transferred to England the possession of New France.

These military settlements, however (if they may be so called), made but little impression on Essex County, and it was only in 1765 (six years after the French were driven from the lake) that a permanent settlement was established. This was effected by William Gilliland, the pioneer proper of Essex. Mr. Gilliland was a wealthy merchant of Irish descent residing in the city of New York. Conceiving the idea of forming a baronial estate in the "dreary wilds of Lake Champlain, then almost a hundred miles from any Christian neighborhood" (as he phrased it in his memorial to Congress in 1777), he purchased a tract of 2,000 acres south of the Boquet River, now distinguished as the Field Patent, and established ("after near twelve years' expense and applica-

tion ") a colony of ninety persons, chiefly Irish,
naming the spot Milltown. In June, 1765, the
first dwelling between Crown Point and Canada
was erected at Willsborough Falls, in the settlement, Mr. Gilliland fixing at the Falls his own
residence. He subsequently purchased more land,
until his estate amounted to 30,000 acres. Here he
lived in Colonial dignity and independence, holding
a Justice's commission, and wielding in fact over the
region the power of a Chief Magistrate, and re-
garded as the sole judicial authority. But the
Revolution broke out, and destroyed his scheme
of baronial power ; Mr. Gilliland, with the true
patriotic spirit which distinguished his life, embracing the cause of his country.

Such were his patriotic exertions, and such his
consequence, that Gen. Carleton, Governor of Canada, offered a reward, in 1775, of five hundred dol-
lars for his capture, and the royal sheriff White, at
the head of a party of Tories and Indians, went in
search of him, but were themselves captured by
him and delivered to Gen. Philip Schuyler.

Unfortunately, however, for him, Lake Champlain offered an easy highway into the State of New
York, and his estate was, consequently, more than
ordinarily exposed. With noble generosity, not-

withstanding, he proffered his means to the friends
of the cause, entertaining from three to four thousand of them, " from the general to the sentinel," at
his own expense, and yielding his rooms to sick officers and soldiers, he sleeping " for weeks together "
on straw. But lying as his estate did, it was
ravaged by friend and foe ; by Benedict Arnold and
Gen. Burgoyne. The Canadian Tories and Indians,
after the surrender of Burgoyne to Gen. Gates, on
their return to Canada swept it with the torch, so
that not a dwelling was left standing. Still he remained the same patriot, devoting every thought to
his country. He it was who in the early stage of
the strife planned the attack of Ticonderoga and
Crown Point, and the capture of the British armed
vessel which held the whole lake in subjection.

But at last, his entire estate disappeared, — from
invasion, litigation, the unfaithfulness of agents and
the robberies of squatters ; and after a confinement
in jail in the city of New York for debt, and in vain
memorializing Congress for assistance, he returned
in 1784 to the settlement, by this time revived.
Failing, however, in his efforts to retrieve his fortunes, with a crazed mind and broken heart, this
true patriot and noble gentleman wandered into
the wilderness alone and died. He was another of

the host of those " of whom the world was not worthy."

In 1775 (May 10) occurred the capture of Ti- conderoga by Col. Ethan Allen, and two days thereafter Crown Point surrendered to Col. Seth Warner.

The first principal scenes of Burgoyne's expe- dition happened in Essex County : the encampment of that general on the banks of the Boquet where he made his memorable speech to his Indian allies, advising against indiscriminate slaughter ; then his triumphal sweep up the lake ; his ascent of Mount Defiance ; capture of Ticonderoga, and subsequent voyage to Skenesboro (now Whitehall).

Close to the north line of Essex occurred, in 1776, the naval battle between Benedict Arnold and Gen. Carleton, at the strait between Valcour Island and the west shore. But of all to remind the visitor now of warlike scenes in Essex County, the roman- tic ruins of Fort Ticonderoga, upon their green head- land, alone exist. There they linger grim and silent, with the summer sunlight goldening and the winter snow-drifts whitening the black remains. The sun- set shoots its red dart into the gloom of the " bakery," and the moonlight, pouring through the openings, pearls the esplanade of grass where the spotting flock and grouping herd slumber.

In 1801 the first manufacture of iron in the county was commenced at Willsborough Falls.

In April 1807 Elizabethtown was made by act the county seat, and seven years afterward, on the completion of the proper buildings, the Court-house and Clerk's Office were removed to the village.

The county is divided into eighteen townships, and has twenty villages and hamlets. The chief villages are Keeseville, Essex, Elizabethtown, Westport, Crown Point, and Ticonderoga.

The Plattsburgh and Whitehall Railroad is now in progress of construction, and will probably be soon completed, thus opening the county as with a golden wand.

The water privileges of the county are unsurpassed. Every stream dashes, calling in loud tones for the mill-wheel, — Ti Stream alone furnishing water-power equal to any other stream in the world.

Three fourths of the soil are too rough and broken for cultivation, but filled, as shown, with sources of wealth, asking development from industry and enterprise.

The manufacture of iron is the leading pursuit of the county, the principal iron works being at Port Henry, Crown Point, Keeseville, Westport, Elizabethtown, and Schroon, while manifold lesser works are scattered all over the district.

There are also manufactories of starch, paper, graphite or black lead, and glass; likewise plank roads — those railroads of the sequestered village and farm — and tanneries, mines of prosperity to the wild regions where they stand.

But of all the wonders and objects of interest in Essex, the most wonderful and interesting object is the one which composes the main title of the following work. It stands prominently forth in grandeur, not only in the County of Essex and State of New York, but on the Continent of America. Mount Marcy is likewise a wonder — the sublime heart of the county, as the county is the sublime mountain-heart of New York, pouring its arteries of waters on every side throughout the Empire State. East of the Rocky Mountains, Tahawus lifts his towering crest among the cloudy summits of the nation.

I close with an extract from the "Geological Report" of the late Professor Emmons, — writing of course as regards the country this side the Rocky Mountains, — the reference in the extract being to the Indian (or as he terms it the Adirondack) Pass : —

"In viewing this great precipice," he observes, "no feeling of disappointment is felt in consequence of the expectation having exceeded the reality. The conception of this imposing mass of rock necessarily falls greatly short of what is experienced when it comes to be seen."

After a description of the feelings engendered by the view from its summit, he proceeds : —

" In conclusion, I remark, that I should not have occupied so much space for the purpose of describing merely a natural curiosity, were it not for the fact that probably in this country there is no object of the kind on a scale so vast and imposing as this. We look upon the Falls of Niagara with awe and a feeling of our insignificance ; but much more are we impressed with the great and the sublime in the view of the simple naked rock of the Adirondack Pass." [1]

---

[1] The cause of the two Indian names of the Pass for the same thing (Otne-yar-heh, Stonish Giants, and Ga-nos-gwah, Giants clothed with Stone) is found in the different dialects of the nations composing the Iroquois Confederacy. The Otne-yar-heh were descended from a family that lived on the east side of the Mississippi River (about twelve hundred and fifty years before Columbus discovered America), and were separated by the breaking of the vine stretching across the river. They became cannibals, acquired a stony skin by rolling in the sand, grew to giants, and invaded the Iroquois, slaying and devouring them. At length the Holder of the Heavens interfered, and, assuming the shape of a giant, pretended to lead the Otne-yar-heh against the Iroquois. He however decoyed them into a deep hollow at night, and at dawn overwhelmed them with a mass of rocks, only one escaping to announce the fate of his companions.

In addition to the other Indian names of the Pass, is this: DA-YOH-JE-GA-GO. *The place where the storm clouds meet in battle with the Great Serpent.* The following wild legend is explanatory of the name: The Evil Spirit of the Iroquois created all things that destroy the life of mankind, among which were the Great Beaver; the Great Bear; Giants clothed with stone; the Great Partridge, whose drumming killed all that heard it; the Great Leech and the Great Serpents which revel in the deep waters, in the dark deep gorges, and beneath the surface of the earth. He-no (Lightning) sends his bolts whenever the serpents are near the surface, and by this means kills them or drives them back to their deep hiding-places. In order to gain more force, He-no employs oftentimes two great clouds as if using both hands.

As well as to Mr. Watson, the writer's obligations are owing to Dr. George T. Stevens; to B. C. Butler, in his *History of Lake George and Lake Champlain ;* and to the *Geological Report* of the late Professor Ebenezer Emmons, on the Second District of the State. The highest honors are due the memory of this great Scientist for his invaluable labors in first making known the mountain system of Northern New York.

THE INDIAN PASS;

OR,

A TRAMP THROUGH THE TREES.

———◆———

CHAPTER I.

THE INDIAN PASS.

The Five Mountain Ranges of Northern New York. — The Departure. — Tramp to the Pass.

FIVE parallel mountain ranges traverse the State of New York in a northeasterly direction, terminating either at Lake Champlain, or in the plains of Canada. The most easterly range rises north of Saratoga Springs, and runs northeasterly through the southeast portion of Warren, and northwest corner of Washington counties. Passing between lakes George and Champlain, it terminates on the latter lake a little south of Ticonderoga. This is called the Black Mountain Range.

The second range, immediately west of the preceding, rises in Montgomery County, and runs parallel with Lake George, which lies to the west,

1

and terminates near Crown Point and Port Henry, on Lake Champlain. It is called the Kayadarosseras Range. The highest peak is Pharaoh Mountain, at Lake Pharaoh in Schroon.

The third range rises north of Johnstown, in the County of Fulton, and, traversing Warren County, terminates on Lake Champlain, at Split Rock. It is known as the East Moriah Range. Crane Mountain is the highest point.

The fourth begins in Montgomery County, and terminates at Willsborough, on Lake Champlain. It averages about nine miles in width, and is distinguished as the West Moriah, or Boquet Range. The highest mountain is Dix's Peak.

The fifth and last range begins at Little Falls, in the County of Herkimer, and, passing through Hamilton County, terminates at Trembleau Point, on Lake Champlain. It is known as the Clinton, or Adirondack Range.

The loftiest portion of this range is a nearly circular group, called the Adirondacks, consisting of Mount Marcy or Tahawus [1] (central and highest), with Mounts Colden and McIntyre, Wallface, Mounts Robertson, Henderson, Seward, and Santanoni, at the west; Boreas Mountain on the south; Haystack, the Dial or Nipple Top, and the Gothics, at the east; with Whiteface north and Blue Mountain south as outposts.

[1] An Indian word, meaning, literally, HE SPLITS THE SKY.

All these mountains, except Mount Seward and Blue Mountain, belong to the County of Essex, the former being in Franklin County and the latter in Hamilton.

The whole five ranges also pass through Essex County; but it is the Adirondack group with which we have to do.

It is of hypersthene formation, fashioned into conical peaks, and sharp, serrated ridges.

It is a strange, weird, and almost unknown region, weltering in the wildest, most impenetrable forests; a region of snows, land-slides, water-spouts, terrific tempests, tornadoes, windfalls, and earthquakes. It is full of horrible gorges, dizzy cliffs, impervious fastnesses, green dingles, lovely lakes, rivers, grassy glades, waterfalls, beautiful beaver-meadows, purling streamlets; and abounds in bears, wolves, deer, panthers, and (but unfrequently and in the wildest places) moose.

Four gorges, peerless in majesty and awful beauty, frown within them. The Indian Pass, the Panther Gorge of Mount Marcy, the Clove or Notch of Whiteface, and the gorge between the Dial and Dix's Peak.

These spots it was my determination to explore, including a visit to lakes Colden and Avalanche; all, with the exception of the Dial gorge, on my way over Mount Marcy to the lovely valley of

Keene. It was necessary to perform the whole journey on foot, — the trail lying through the wildest and most inaccessible forests of the Adirondacks, portions of which were almost unknown. The trail was of the faintest description, only to be followed by the most experienced woodmen, — touching along the ridges and etching the hollows, eked out by the runways of wolf and panther, as well as deer. For miles it was merely a bear-track. I should thus welter day after day in the sea-like wilderness where broken lights only entered, and where the moss stood undisturbed even by the breath of the tempest, so close and impervious were the depths. To say I looked forward to this journey with interest, would convey but a slight idea of my sensations. The wildest romance tinged my dreamings, and the liveliest curiosity spurred me on in my anticipations. To see the forest — the real, primeval, mysterious forest, where axe never rung save the hunter's, or roof never rose but the shanty of brush and saplings; the great, stretching, splendid wilderness; to be buried alive in its fastnesses, and feel its influence in my innermost soul — this was the impulse of my nature, the warm desire of my heart. I had with all my wanderings, I was conscious, never seen this forest. True I had floated through the woods over sheltered waters, and encamped on points, islands, and shores of leafy beauty; but I had only hovered (save in my trip to the Beaver waters of the St. Regis) at its extremities. The vast, dark, deep heart I had really never seen. I was now to pierce into the deepest recesses of this heart, open up its secrets, and revel in its grandeur and beauty.

The time had now arrived for this contemplated tramp, and I consequently made preparations for the long, fatiguing, but most unique and exciting journey of over eighty miles. Truly a most glorious tramp through a most magnificent region.

As it was very necessary to have guides familiar with the Adirondacks, I determined to engage a couple at Scott's on the Elizabethtown Road, about ten miles from the Lower Saranac Lake, and which I also resolved to make my point of departure.

Accordingly, at ten o'clock, one bright September day, I found myself at Scott's, ten miles due north from the Indian Pass. Here I hired two guides, Loyal A. Merrill and Robert Scott Blin, for the entire trip; and faithful, reliable guides I found them, and would commend them most heartily to all disposed to make the journey which I, under their auspices, accomplished.

I passed the day at this most quiet and beautiful spot in completing still farther my arrangements, and in surveying the localities. The place smiles an oasis of meadow and grain-field, in the midst of mountain forests. Looking south, the dizzy pyramid of Mount McIntyre rises most splendidly green from base to brow, with a smaller mountain leaning upon its breast like a bride. Indeed, gazing through my opera-glass, I thought, in the mist with which the whole scene was at first shrouded, the latter was McIntyre, until raising my glass still higher, I saw a background that filled the glass the higher I raised it, until lo! the summit was gained, and there stood the magnificent mass, like a stupendous thunder-cloud. It was most impressive, yea, it was truly awful, my first view of Mount McIntyre. The opening of the Indian Pass between this grand mountain and Wallface, is clearly perceptible, veiling itself in softest azure, the latter rounding down like the "bended beak" of the eagle. How different, this velvet sweetness of tint, this melting blandness of look, from the stern, gray, cracked; startling crag that walls the Pass, none could appreciate, but those who had seen its horrors. West, over the huge rampart or bastion of Wallface, which mountain curves north to within a mile or two of Scott's, peers up the cloven crest of Mount Seward. East of McIntyre stands a cone of blue, so faint, a breeze would seemingly dissolve it into the summer heaven ; yet there frowns Mount Colden, the most stern and savage of all the Adirondack group. Frequently it shakes from its rocky sides its robe of forest, tumbling pines and crags like straws and pebbles in thundering chaos at its feet, thus peeling, as it were, in mad wrath, its very flesh from its shuddering frame. The two beautiful lakes Colden and Avalanche, its own children, which it wears like jewels of its sandals, are nearly choked with these fragments of its existence and emblems of its wrath. And there it stands, casting an awe over the very sunshine! here seeming so sweet and smiling!

Next upon its throne of forest, soars exultingly Mount Marcy or Tahawus, the Piercer of the Sky, Monarch of the Mountains, Darer of the Lightning, and Conqueror of the Storm! How soft and smiling too, — a fragment of the soft heaven, soft as the blue of spring's first violet.

Next this King of the Crags, is seen the Dial, supporter of its rocky dome, like Atlas bearing aloft the globe; and close to the Titan scowls the sleeping lion of Dix's Peak. Thence, circling the horizon, swell the summits of the Keene Mountains to where north, the crest of Whiteface blots the sky.

Truly a most glorious frame for this little picture of peace and plenty, this garden-spot of swaying grass and glittering grain.

The morning of my start was bright and beautiful, but warm. Donning my thick, blue hunting-shirt, with a leather belt tightly clasping my waist, and clutching a stout walking-stick, with Irish hobnails in my strong laced shoes, and with my two stalwart guides, bearing. canvas knapsacks of provender, I started joyfully for my first long wished for goal — the Indian Pass. " My eyes make pictures when they're shut," sings Coleridge, and I busied myself in building the terrific wall in my fancy, while following my guides across the sylvan road and over a few rough pastures, due south toward my destination. The sunshine burned kindly upon me, and the occasional flit of a downy breeze was welcome. Crossing the last field, full of curled golden-rods and grouped asters, we came to a wood road, or rather a green vista of the woods.

" Hurrah for the Indian Pass ! " said Robert, the youngest of my guides, a lad of eighteen, with a flourish of his knapsack over his head.

" Hurrah ! " echoed Merrill, my head guide, " hurrah ! "

" Hurra-a-h ! " reëchoed I with a glow at my heart and a more important thrill at my heels.

The vista led south through an open wood, clustered with hopples and whortleberry bushes. We shortly reached the dwelling of Robert's father, and completed an arrangement in the shape of additional loaves of bread, and a " chunk " (Robert's word) of sweet sound pork, and a few more rosy-skinned, carbuncle-eyed peach-blow potatoes. Here I readjusted my shoe — which, I forgot to mention, was framed over the toe and instep of my right foot with copper, to protect the soft, raw flesh consequent upon the recent loss of a nail. The copper pressed upon the bulge of the foot, and fearful of a chafe, I rearranged it, and made it, as far as possible, comfortable for my prospective long, rough, and weary tramp through the forest. I then relaced tightly my shoes, thus harnessing my faithful " team," and we started. Passing over another field or two, we came to the west branch of the Ausable River, flowing among its plentiful pebbles in a wide but shallow channel. A rude scow, propelled by Robert's staff, carried us across the black, swift current, and, ascending the weedy border, we plunged instantly into the wild woods, — woods which immersed us continuously for a fortnight, and which yielded us to the open day only (with the exception of three quiet days I passed at the village of the " Upper Works ") when we emerged into the green, beautiful valley of Keene.

Gratefully did the balm of the forest shadow fall upon me with its emerald gloom and brooding peace. And now began our work. We fell into Indian file, that natural — indeed the only — way of threading the woods, following a faint, narrow trail bushed out only a month previous, by a com-

pany of woodmen (Robert being one), detailed and
led by Scott himself acting as guide.

I could see, with my little forest experience, that
we were now in the deep, tangled wilderness, the
unmistakable woods of the wild, savage Adirondacks:
woods in which the Indian Pass shrouds itself from
the eye of all but the most ardent lovers of the
picturesque; woods where lakes Colden and Avalanche slumber, year after year, with almost no
encroachment from man, wasting their beauty on
the gazing mountains; woods with which the grand
Tahawus wraps his giant shoulders, but in which he
does not suffer his rocky brow to be mantled, crushing them flat in the chill frown of his kingly look.

With a strong consciousness of the labor de-
manded ere I should accomplish my journey, I
pressed forward, trampling the lush wood-plants in
my path, and feeling the delicate steel-like elasticity
of the forest earth lifting my feet as with wings as I
strode. Frequently at first, owing to the awkward-
ness of my copper shoe, I stumbled and pitched,
sometimes on my breast and sometimes on my head,
but with no damage save a deeper " bung " (another
of Robert's words) to my soft felt hat or nightcap,
for my head covering answered both purposes.

Onward, onward! Past colonnades of lordly
trunks, where the sunlight lay in speckles; past
vistas opening denser shades, and looking as if only

the light foot of the rabbit or partridge had ever left a print; past delicious dingles where diamond runlets danced; past hemlocks dripping with ringletted moss as old towers with ivy; past delicate white birches glittering as if of silver in the emerald light; past vast orbs of roots upturned by some old tornado; past huge rocks, green with moss and red with weather stains and lichen, and twined with roots that pines and cedars knotted; past beautiful glades where the blue-joint and silver-weed, aster and golden-rod, grew; past the little rivulet from the mountain-rock, glancing onward, a streak of pearl; past the sapling glued to the tree, and wood-sprout rising to the sapling, and lithe buff stem to the sprout; past the purple hopple and the crimson sumach; past the old log (these logs were abominations in causing "hoist" to the weary legs) weltering in prickly brambles and plumy brake; past light in sprinkles, light in spots, light in dots, and light in sparkles; past shade in nooks, shade in brooks, shade in corners of rocks, and shade in twisted fissures, shade in depth of fir-trees and shade in hearts of bushy cedars; past dead tamaracks, and tamaracks in scattered golden hues; past gray trees forlorn, and desolate and gray trees dying in one another's clutch like fighting deer; past threatening swamps where dead trees decayed; gloomy ravines, frowning hollows, sloping ridges, and

steep acclivities; past graceful arches of foliage
like ranges of Gothic windows, with foliage in
arabesque twined each side like walls; in short,
right through the tameless, wolfy, primeval forest,
we swiftly went. The raven uttered his hoarse
croak as he scented us and floated blackly off; the
partridge reared her mottled crown and scudded
away to the crackle of our footsteps; the deer
" arched its slim neck from glades " to snapping
twigs, and glanced away as its soft black orbs met
our dreaded shapes glimmering from out the green
distance; the bear, pacing and waddling in the trail,
doubtless huddled his furry form into the cleft of
some old log as he heard the strange trample; the
panther lifted his fore-paw with sharp, erected ears,
ceasing, for the moment, his velvet glide o'er the
yielding moss; and the wild wolf stood still with
lifted front as the echoes gave back the careless
whistle or clear halloo of the approaching foes.

On, on we went. As I felt the tire of the
tramp, down I sank in the plump moss, which
clasped me, with a caress; down on the wreathed
root, in the soft fern-filled hollow; and when the
tire melted from my limbs, up again I rose with a
cheery " Hurrah, boys!" thus taking up once more
the dropped thread of trail. Now we rested on
some cushioned rock, and now on some trunk fallen
athwart the track. Now we reached some deep

ravine where the mountain-brook threaded its broad path of pebbles, and in the spattered light sat until the flitting fatigue was over; and now we braced our strength to breast the unfrequent ridge that sloped across our way.

Thus passed the pleasant sylvan hours until the afternoon gleam rested on the western foliage, for by this sign alone knew we the flight of the day over the sky of leaves.

At length we came to a wild clearing lined with bushes.

" Father's sugar place!" said Robert. " We make the tallest kind of maple-sugar here, in the spring! See, the troughs and things are all about!" pointing to a few wooden troughs hollowed rudely by the axe and darkened with the weather, lying around, with here and there a sapling black with smoke, the cranes of the sap-kettles, and the smoke-stained stones, the kitchen-hearth of the "sugar-bush."

It was a wild, forest scene, full now of quiet and sunshine. I fancied, however, the "sugaring" in the spring. The stalwart form of the elder Blin bends over the mammoth black kettles bubbling with the rich tawny liquor, and ladles from one to the other the fast stiffening stuff, attenuating it from his lifted ladle into delicate spider-threads, to see how far it had grained; now he places the hissing, sputtering kettle in the March snowdrift " to cool

off," and now he tastes the contents to see if they
had taken accidentally a " burn." Cakes of sugar
are ranged in brown, tempting rows on nice, clean
barken slabs, ready for use, while the crackling fires
fill the whole maple ridge with rosy comfort ; on the
towering maples, hacks have been made in which are
white spouts from which the sap falls in twinkling
drops into the troughs below, drop, drop, like minute
bells rivaling the carol of the witnessing bluebird.

Before my picture faded, we had crossed the
" bush " and plunged into the opposite forest.

We now came to a path intersecting our trail
from the west, or at our right.

" Eppes's trail to the Pass ! " said Robert, allud-
ing to a well-known guide. Forward again, with
the scenery described continually renewed.

The afternoon gleam crept lower and lower.
" I'll show you at the first beginning of the Pass
the way to the three ponds found out by Mr.
Scott on the highest top of Wallface ! " said Robert. " He was out a moose-hunting, and came
upon them forty years ago! They send out
streams, according to his tell, every way. The one
that comes out here away is one of the sprouts to
the west branch of the Ausable River. Another
goes into Cold River, running west into Racket
River, nigh Long Lake, and another goes down into
Lake Henderson and is one of the branches of old

Hudson. The three ponds are jined together way up nigh the top of Wallface. They've never been seen but by Scott, and a good many folks say there aint no such ponds. But I believe Mr. Scott, and he says so. A good many folks, guides too, git lost turning up this way ; that is, before this trail was ' bushed out,' thinking it the way to the Pass. They get awfully taken in, though. It's an awful sort of a place to get into, and that's the reason nobody could get to the ponds after Scott. There was a guide turned up here, supposing he was on the way to the Pass, with a gentleman, and got lost, and both like to have starved to death, besides being tuckered out. At last, however, after roaming about two or three days, they stumbled back, and made tracks towards Scott's, glad enough to get out alive from the awful old woods. Lord save me from being lost in them ! "

As this was the evidence of a woodman, born in the woods and knowing nothing else, despising the hardships and steeled to their dangers, I thought no higher testimonial could be furnished to the utter savagery of these tremendous forests, should a devi-ation from the faithful compass-trail be unhappily made. I thought and shuddered.

Gladly I turned to another theme. I fancied a picture of these lonely goblets of Wallface, hiding on the top of the tall mountain, overrunning with these three streams, — mountain-torrents dashing down from ledge to ledge, through rocky gorge and leafy ravine, to link their pure, bright waters with the fierce Ausable, the gentle Racket, and the mighty Hudson that bends his vassal-knee to none but Ocean.

A gray glimmer now broke through the stems, and the next moment we descended the border of a wide-channeled brook strewed with white pebbles, rocks, and mossy boulders, through which struggled threads of sable water flecked in spots with foam.

It was the west branch of the Ausable River. Born in the Indian Pass, it bids eternal adieu to its twin the Hudson, and goes onward, strengthening as it goes, disdaining barriers, and fainting not to thirsty suns that fain would exhaust its struggling life, until it leaps in white, live lightning through the Clove of Whiteface, and rolling in its course, a river, and shaping at its wild will the beautiful Keene Valley, it links at last with the eastern branch, and flows in braided and songful peace through grain and grass, until it mingles with the broad mirror of Lake Champlain.

We crossed the stream upon the scattered rocks, and, ascending the opposite bank, found a beautiful little bough-house in a leafy nook, into which we gladly stretched ourselves after our long and weary tramp.   We were now but two miles from the great Pass whose breath, even at this distance, we felt in the increased chilliness of the atmosphere. After a short rest, I went down to the river for a draught of its cool, delicious nectar, and, through the vista of the channel, lo ! the Indian Pass in a rough, grotesque outline of crag, smiting the sunset, and clutching at a rosy cloud as if to cast it into the terrific chasm at its feet.

I looked long at this first glimpse of the monster that had so long lifted its weird wall, its magic battlement, its mighty bastion in these far away forests, unknown, and unvisited. Here was my first sight of the rocky giant, the grand Titan of the Adirondacks.

The fine light of the first sunset now goldened the air, and we made preparations to sup by its transparent torch. Merrill caught a delicate trout or two from the Ausable, to which Robert added a squirrel and the white saddle of a frog. Tea soon sent its spicy fragrance in the soft air, the camp-fire winked from under a leafy arch, the feathery fern offered us a couch on which to recline, Roman fashion, while partaking our meal, and the whole was so pleasant and sylvan, that I wished my home lay in this

" Boundless contiguity of shade."

After a pipe or two, and listening to the song of the Ausable to its pebbles, we left the bough-house

2

for an hour's tramp nearer the Pass, and then to spend the night at its northeast portals.

Whereas the route ran throughout the day through an agreeable interchange of ridge and hollow, the ground now began rapidly to ascend. We were evidently approaching the lair of the gray monster, whose size is thus in some measure dwarfed by the magnitude and grandeur of the scene around him.

The gold tinge darkened into tawny, the leaves commenced to mingle, the trunks to lose their sharp outlines as we approached the camping spot for the night. It was a little leafy dingle we selected for our bough-house to be built in, and, reaching it, I sank on the moss, while Merrill prepared to erect our woodland shelter. First, he scanned the spot : then he seized the axe. A sapling fell to his blow and a few cuts transformed it into a forked pole about four feet in height, which he planted in the earth. Soon, a corresponding pole stood by its neighbor, about six feet apart. Then another pole, from a slender sapling, was laid transverse in the forks, and lo, the front of the simple structure ! Hack, hack, hack ! and other poles unforked are cut and planted at the sides. Two long saplings are laid within the forks above the ridge-pole, and slanted downward to a mound of moss. Poles are then placed along for the roof, caught by the ends of the side poles standing five or six inches above the downward slanted ones, and the light skeleton of the shanty is completed. Merrill then shears long and thick hemlock branches, and piles them on the roof, and trims them at the sides, and the beautiful little shanty is finished. No! for spruce-fringes are needed to strew and soften the floor into a couch of elastic and fragrant " three-ply," and the little structure is fitted to be an hotel for the night. And thus I watched it as it rose like a mushroom from the soil, or a bubble from a trout's maw, in all its cunning yet simple workmanship.

The dusk thickened. The white stars palpitated out; night reigned, and silence also. The stately forests waving in the evening breath seemed fanning themselves into slumber. No sound but the Ausable: no sign of life but ourselves: no light but the camp-fire.

The dusk is now blank darkness. The white stars are golden. Silence deepens. The fanning leaves are still. Louder the Ausable murmurs. Redder the camp-fire shines.

> " Hark, from the Pass a ringing cry!
>   Is it the panther prowling there?
> And list the low wind's rising sigh!
>   And what weird shapes the branches wear!
> How hushed the utter solitude!
>   Nature herself seems buried here!
> And what deep quiet seems to brood!
>   How echo seems to listen near!'"

Portentous muttering tones came on the chilly gusts from the Pass, as if the spirits of the night were sallying abroad from their rocky home, mingling their murmurs with the voice of the monster. " Listen, mortal!" that voice seemed to say; "why disturb me in my solitude! Why bring the cares and sorrows of life here in my calm woods, lapt as I am in my serene peace. The Creator built me up in the quiet heavens, as if to rear me nearer His divine presence, and exempt me from the troubles of humanity. Vain thought! Notwithstanding the depth of my solitude, I cannot live in peace. Avaunt, mortal, or dread my wrath!"

I listened, and as I did so, a terrific gust burst from the cavernous and mighty Pass, like a demon's shout. Low bowed the trees; the forest shuddered to its depth. And lo! riding on the gust, forth streamed a sable cloud right from the gloom of the Pass, as if to warn and daunt the daring intruders upon his solitude. Again, and hark! a growl of thunder like the voice of a rousing lion also from the gorge. A storm is rising in its bosom, and will burst in terror soon along the forest! Another peal, and now a glance of lightning! I had long felt the presence of the Pass. I knew it stood looming over my head, albeit my eye saw it not in the darkness. But now, to the red flit of the tempest's eye, the gray crag started out with a savage, witch-like, wolf-like glare, as if seeking me for its victim; but it flashed for a moment, and with its light, out gleamed the sable clouds, the sabler chasm, and the shivering trees. The next, it shrank again within the gloom. Another growl, another glance! Once more the gray, cracked, awful cliff gleamed redly out, seeming the guardian demon of the spot, dashing aside for an instant his raven cloak, to show his horrible brow to the stranger shuddering at his portals. Another peal and flash; but by this time I became so confoundedly sleepy, and finding I was not devoured body and bones (according to Robert), I let my head sink upon my moundy pillow, and in a few moments I was asleep.

Again I woke. Holy quiet steeped the forests. Brightest blue clothed the heavens. Full in their naked midst, round, clear, and golden-eyed, beamed the blessed moon! Hushed was the jarring storm. No more the lightning flitted. No more the thunder rolled. Sweet and high in the glowing blue soared the gray, mighty cliff, gleaming like silver in the angelic moonlight. The dread, black, frowning scene was transmuted into the smiling, soft, and dreamy picture, and once more I resigned myself to slumber.

CHAPTER II.

THE INDIAN PASS.

The Indian Pass. — The Upper Works. — Iron Ore Beds. — Lake Henderson. — The Blast Furnace. — Lake Sanford.

THE dawn was sketching faint outlines as I once more opened my eyes. The camp-fire was almost dead. The shanty was breathing out its damp perfume like a bouquet. The song of the Ausable was loud, and the wandering bugles of the blue jays were frequent in the thickets.

Our frugal breakfast over, in which the mealy peach-blow and the fresh, sweet, crispy trout were conspicuous with the nectarean tea, and we pointed our steps toward the Pass. And now stern work was before us! Up, up, up we clambered by the ladder of roots ; up, up, up, by the notches of ledges ; still up, clinging to the crevice, laboring up the detached rock, swung high up by the hemlock's elastic plumage. Breathless, at last, we reach the level ground, and selah ! soaring in stately front magnificent, rises the dizzy cliff. Exultant it hails the morning ! But I hardly allow myself a glance, for the prospect from the brow of the grim crag invites me before I study the grand picture from below. So we cross the gorge, including the narrow channel of the Ausable, and address ourselves to scaling the lesser precipice, one thousand feet in air. Child's play proved the late clambering. Up, straight almost as the tamarack's stem, up, up we scrambled. Now we hung by the root, now drew ourselves by the branch to precarious foothold in the fissure. The few grassy platforms we met, bore aloft tall plumes of pines; and now and then we uncovered, by the tearing up of grass tuft and mossy cushion, the birthplace of the fountain. At last, after a most harassing clamber, we reached a " wind-slash " — a jumble of fallen trees tangling a steep ravine, a perfect net of prostrate trunks and branches. Up, up we tore, until we reached a knotted log lifted above the "jam," and impending over an abyss. Clinging to the bulges and antlers of this hanging bridge we crept our precarious way along it, but refrained from glance at the gorge, reserving this until we should attain our perch at the summit of the rock to which the bridge led. At last we reached the point, and paused a moment to inhale full, deep breaths. We knew a sublime and terrible sight awaited us. We turned and looked. A shudder shook my frame. My eyes swam, my brain grew dizzy. Instinctively I clung nearer the cliff, for we were in a down-sloping niche of the mighty wall, and I grasped closer the branch I had clutched above me, and thrust deeper my foot into the crevice beneath. After a few moments of thus bracing my system and recovering from the first sickening shock, I again looked. What a sight! horrible and yet sublimely beautiful — no, not beautiful; scarce an element of beauty there — all grandeur and terror.

Right in front sloped with grand breast of fleecy woods, touched with autumn tints (one beautiful feature), Mount McIntyre, plunging from his height of five thousand feet, and distinctly visible from his brow but not to base, down, down, past my sight into the awful chasm below. Down, down, close under me and at either hand, fell the sheer precipice on the brow of which I was perched, plunging also into the black abyss, so black, so deep, it seemed as if the earth had yawned and stood with sable throat to swallow me. The indescribable crawl of the nerves, felt only in the most dangerous situations, thrilled my whole system. I had the insane desire, the almost irresistible impulse, to throw myself headlong into the chasm. Merrill tore a large stone from the cliff and hurled it. So deep the chasm that gravitation seemed suspended, for, notwithstanding its weight, the stone wavered like a wounded bird ere, plunging below, it was ost to the eye. No sound of its smiting the floor of the gorge followed. The distance was too great to allow the echo to be heard.

Immediately at our right, the picturesque profile of the wall, where it soared from the thousand feet of our level a half thousand more into the sky, looked grim and threatening, the outlines twisted into the semi-likeness of a man, or rather the whole likeness of a grinning demon.

At last, the wild picture being ingrained, or rather sunk like an intaglio into my memory, there to remain forever, we prepared to descend. And first, to withdraw from our dangerous and precarious perch ! Leaving one pendent branch to clutch another, unclasping our foothold from one crevice to insert it quickly into a second, we turned round, and drew ourselves cautiously upward until we reached again the level brow of the precipice. Fighting through the ghastly labyrinth of the " slash," we plunged downward toward the gorge. Down, down the steep side of the rocky wall, pendulumizing (excuse the word) ourselves over the chasm, and scrambling down the ravine, we reached what appeared a " short cut " to the bottom of the gorge. It was a fearfully steep earthen channel, or rather throat, the bed of some torrent with rough sheer banks. Merrill descended a short way, but the throat became so suddenly steep, that his footfall slipped from under him, and he only saved himself by clinging to a friendly hand a hemlock stretched to him from the bank. Well for him was it so, for a few rods farther would have carried him over a sheer precipice of three or four hundred feet into the gorge. Clutching the hanging boughs of the bordering hemlocks, the stout guide at length reascended to where we stood watching his descent and trembling for his safety.

At last, after most fatiguing efforts, we stood again on the path of the gorge. After successfully performing this feat of ascent, which as far as I am able to learn had seldom before been achieved, we recrossed the Ausable, regained the dark slope of Mount McIntyre, and prepared to thread the awful Pass to its head.

Although, as before, I felt the presence of the impending wall, so close grew the trees on the slope and in the gorge, we were sensible only of a lofty outline glimmering brokenly high up at our right. Nature seemed determined to hide her splendid wonder from unhallowed gaze, even when the adventurer's foot had annihilated the space she had interposed between it and the world.

At our right rose enormous, rough rocks, green with moss, and plumed with stately trees, completely, to all appearance, blocking the gorge.

On, on we struggled, Mount McIntyre sloping
up, up, high beyond our gaze, on our left, until
we arrived where we could cross to a rock which
reared a steep craggy pinnacle in the midst of the
gorge. It was the "lookout" place. Clambering its rough sides with difficulty, we reached the
top, and from it an unobstructed view of the wall
opened from head to foot in all its appalling
majesty. Its shape is that of a half-moon curving
outwardly, a mighty bastion. Directly from below
us sprang the gray furrowed wall, with a débris of
loose rocks, looking like mere pebbles, piled five
hundred feet at its base, and soaring upward till
it seemed it might catch the very clouds floating
over it. The grand sight took away the breath,
like an ascent in a balloon. The eye grew dizzy
in struggling up, up, to master its height. It appeared almost like surmounting the battlements of
heaven, — as if the monster had been obliged to
break an opening through the sky to rear its horrible brow to its full altitude. Let it be remembered, also, that the bottom of the gorge, the lair
of the monster, was lifted eighteen hundred feet
above the sea level, and some idea might be gained
of the fearful and crushing height. Although
this was the loftiest point of the Pass, yet far
northward, with scarce less height, on waved and
surged the wall, cutting the blue with a sharp,

jagged sky-line. It was a magnificent spectacle, worthy the great God whose finger had ploughed it. Evidently it had not been formed by the rending asunder of Wallface and McIntyre, but was an original creation as much as the mountains themselves, riveted by Nature to old Wallface — a splendid cuirass, an enormous breastplate — as if to repel the threatened attack of its opposite mountain-foe, should he attempt the thunderbolt of a land-slide against him.

We descended from our perch to the bottom of the gorge. If the precipice appeared lofty from the rock, how it sprang exultingly from the gorge's floor to smite, far, far upward, the highest heavens! And what a chaos around me! Black cedars, like the bristling hairs of a moose's mane, covered the floor, and tottered from the tops of the fallen cliffs, which were of height themselves sufficient to chain the eye in any other place. Far above, on the face of the cracked wall, enormous fissures and cavities frowned blackly, showing whence the rocks had fallen, loosened either by age, earthquakes, or by the mighty agency of fires in ages past, sweeping furnace-like along, shriveling and withering the trees, and fracturing the mighty crag. Down, deep down trickled a blind rill, mining like a mole through a narrow tunnel of the broken, jagged rocks, and I knew it was the infant

Hudson whose birthplace oozed from the gashed heart of the monster, thus blending at last the fragrance of the mountain juniper with the briny odor of old Ocean. Like the intertwining of the fingers of the human hand, the slender source of the Ausable also oozed from the mighty gorge, and, almost braiding their glancing streaks, the two rivers, parting at length on the water-shed of the gorge, started upon their long journeys in entirely different ways, — the bright Hudson through the southwestern portals of the Pass, and the dark Ausable through the northeastern. How many brothers thus start in life from the same hearth, and continue in divergent paths till death.

Winding and struggling on our way through the spruces, and rocky fragments upon the gorge's floor, we saw huge apertures formed by the piled-up rocks, which stood, some on edge, others slanting sidewise, as if a breath could set them rolling; great sable caverns in which scores of panthers could be hidden; bear's nests, wolf-dens without number. It seemed unnatural that some wild animal should not spring from them upon us, or at least the red sparkle of his eyeballs should not glance from out the gloomy depths. Panther, bear, wolf might have been there as far as we knew, for we were not owls enough to trust our precious carcasses in those " skeery places." " No," said Robert, "not if we were out of pork and beans and going in would give us a bushel full!" And I thought with him. There was one cavity, however, we did go into. That was the famous "Ice Cavern." Down, down, very far down, in depths whence a chilly breath uprose, pale, ghastly fragments gleamed like skeletons, which turned out blocks of ice, unmelted in August, and which had never felt the warmth of a summer's sun. All the panthers of the Adirondacks — and they are legion — are entirely welcome to that hole.

Threading our course still deeper, the cradle of the Hudson was passed, and a tinkle, deep in the seams and furrows of the gorge, was heard — the song of the infant river. Another tinkle was mingled, the voice of the Ausable. Soft and low sounded the music, different from the hoarse thunder of the latter through the rended rocks of Whiteface, or the splintering earthquake peals of the former, when with a Titan's struggle he bursts his icy prison in March, making his shores quake and hearts in cities tremble.

At the northeast portal, just where the Ausable (or Notch-Stream, as it is sometimes called) bends downward in a course of forty miles ere it reaches Lake Champlain, descending, in that short distance, twice the fall of the Mississippi in its two thousand, lurks another ice cavern, according to Robert, but which escaped me, owing to the fatigue of the ascent.

The day glided quickly onward in our explorations, and sunset was now jeweling the Pass with its gemmy colors. We made our way once more toward the north portal of the Pass, having determined to spend another night there in the bough-house, and the next morning start anew on our tramp. We soon came to the little leafy shanty, and having supped on several of the golden trout of the Ausable, caught in the low light of the sunset, we, as the night fell darkly around, addressed ourselves to our welcome slumbers.

At midnight I was awakened by a terrific storm of thunder and lightning, accompanied by bursts of blasts that shook the scene almost like an earthquake. I found the two mountains in ,furious altercation, one answering the other, as if about to engage in mortal strife. As I listened, the sounds shaped themselves into words.

"Ho!" roared the towering McIntyre, "why am I thus disturbed! Cease that voice of thine, O Wallface, or dread my wrath."

"Ho, ho!" thundered Wallface in his turn, "dost thou threaten? Cease thyself, thy silly clamor, or dread *my* wrath."

"What!" said the mighty McIntyre, and as he spoke an angry glare of lightning kindled all his awful form that was offered to my gaze, playing around his head as if he were darting red glances at his foe ; " this, slave, to me — me, who could crush thee with my might as my slides crush the rocks in their pathway ? "

" Thou crush me, proud mountain — me, whose craggy breastplate hath dashed back a thousand storms, and against which centuries have gnawed in vain ! Thou crush me ! ho, ho, silly thing, thou provokest me to laughter ! " and a blast thundered from Wallface that seemed to make him shake like the pine-tree in the wind.

" Thing, thing ! " repeated McIntyre, and a second glare of lightning suffused his summit, causing it to leap from the darkness, and stand flashing in the intolerable blaze. " Now will I hurl my mighty crags against thee, until I crumble thee into pebbles at my feet. What is thy boasted breastplate to me ? Lo, I will rend it as the panther rends the deer ! " and again the crimson torrent of the storm displayed him reared in his terrific fury, as if indeed to make good at the very moment his boast.

" Ho, ho ! " laughed hoarsely again Wallface, " what care I for thy crags ! Cease thy vaunts, thou braggart, and seek again thy rest. Thou rend my breastplate ! Lo, I will cast myself against thee with this same breastplate full of rocky points, and pierce and crush thee until thou tumblest from thy couch to the gorge beneath thee ! " and a third cataract of lightning, accompanied by a launch of thunder that made my heart bound within me, displayed the vast segment of the precipice next my eye fluttering as it were in the light, as if it at all events would dash itself against the kingly form of the foe.

"Ha!" said McIntyre, "thou wilt come, wilt thou? Come, then, and find thyself broken to pieces in the contact! Ho, ho, ho! slave, poor, puny object, tremble and leave me to my repose, or I will this instant crush thee into the very earth, from which, in my royal presence, thou shouldst never have arisen."

At this awful juncture the wild storm arrived at its height, with a perfect flood of rain. Onward dashed the blasts like ocean billows, wreaths of lightning blazed, and rolls of thunder shook the scene, while both mountains roused now to the utmost pitch of frenzy, roared and howled as if they had indeed met and were struggling in deadly grapple. Frequently grand shocks of falling rocks made the gorge groan and tremble, and I listened in shuddering dismay. My soul broke out into the demoniac strife of the elements: it soared with the blasts, rioted with the lightning, launched away with the thunder, and mingled with the warfare of the mountains. It seemed as if I were swayed by insanity. But suddenly the strife ceased, the storm strode off, the mountains grew calm, and the tor-

3

tured scene was silent. Out broke the moon, the seraph of the night, and I sank once more upon my fragrant couch. But far away through the quiet crept a dulcet sound, the sound of the dying wind, like the wail of the *Miserere* through the cathedral aisle. " Rest, mortal ! " it sang in sweetest cadence ; " the tempest is past, and the peace of the night now surrounds thee ! Rest, and thank thy God that He is ever near to fold thee to His bosom, and bid thee sleep in safety ! "

I heard and blessed Him, as the Friend and Father ! blessed Him as my Creator, Preserver, and Benefactor, while into my deepest heart thrilled anew the *Miserere*, the wail of a soul broken for its sin.

How often have I listened to that chaunt ! Swelling like the wind-swept pine, how the choral voices mingle ! the sweet tenor, the lordly bass, and the tender treble, with one fine tone piercing through the rest, and ringing along the dusky arches of the Cathedral Temple !

The morning rose over the earth, calm as an infant's breath and bright as a maiden's eye. And the two mountains ! — how different from the wrath of the night before ! Why, they looked sleek and innocent as two Quakers. I wouldn't have supposed they had ever sent a growl, or uttered a threat. McIntyre smiled at Wallface, and the latter returned the smile. Two cooing doves were the fierce old mountains : I almost thought they would embrace each other.

" Ho, brother ! " said Wallface, " thou wert somewhat angry with me yesternight ! Why, I really thought at one time thou wert in earnest."

" And I, brother, thought at one time that thou wert inclined a little to scold," returned the amiable McIntyre, fanning himself with a fluttering aspen ; " but I forgive thee ! "

" And I thee, O kingly McIntyre," said the equally amiable Wallface. " But it was all of that saucy lightning and thunder. I must confess the storm did burn me a little, with its red sparks, while the thunder touched the tympanum of my ear somewhat rudely. Besides, the little puff of wind gave me a passing brush somewhat rudely."

" Confound the wind ! " said McIntyre, " I felt a brush of it too ! It sent a cold streak straight down my shoulder. But it is over now, and we dwell hereafter in unity and peace."

Till the next storm comes, thought I. What a horrible caterwauling these two brothers must keep up during the winter ! Why there is probably no more peace for the surrounding region than for the inmates of Bedlam. As for the poor Gorge lying between the two, tears of compassion are due it.

Onward anew through the pass. Flutterings of

white on the precipice's face, like mist, or the wings of doves, told the manifold waterfalls, while now and then a stern, deep shock of sound spoke of some fragment falling from the cliff to the floor of the gorge. All was weird and sublime, so entirely differing from ordinary sights and sounds as to remove the scene up into the regions of the fanciful and magical.

At length we stood at the southwest portal of the Pass, where the broad breastplate of rock forming the precipice, bending slightly southward and suddenly dropping, clutched with gray rivets the mountain's flank, and became lost in the verdure of the common soil.

As far from this point as the eye reached, breaking up the southwest horizon as if a mighty sea was there tumbling, the summits of Mounts Robertson, Henderson, Santanoni, and Seward startled the sight, deepening in their sweet, fairy azure the farther they retreated, until they melted to a misty dream. There lay, I knew, the three Preston Ponds, fountains among others of the Racket River, and gemming the sandals of Mount Seward, Mountain of the White Star (whose peaks were hidden by Wallface), at the north, and the crests of Santanoni on the south, with the silver wand also of Cold River between the two, — as if the ponds and their tiny silver staff had cloven them asunder. At the

southeast were clustered, I also knew, the dozen
roofs of the "Upper Works," or "Adirondack
Village." Far beyond, a lily-wreathed basin deep
in the weltering woods proclaimed the outlet of
Lake Henderson. Woods, woods, woods — nothing
but woods. What a lair for the monster Pass. A
lair of ten miles to Scott's, north; five miles to the
Upper Works, south; fifteen miles to Long Lake,
southwest; and thirty miles over Mount Tahawus
to the Keene Valley, east; all one deep tangled
wilderness, where the axe of the settler has never
sounded since Creation.

This prospect from the gorge was splendid
though wild; savage in its beauty like a panther.
A weary tramp still lay before us in the sunset
ere we reached the grassy hamlet of the Upper
Works, and before starting we crouched by a
fountain of dark glass, — a mere drinking-cup, a
goblet in the gorge, — to brew our tea. It was the
first basin of the Hudson. Why a hopple-leaf
could not much more than float there, and yet
that water foamed fifty leagues away under the
keels of myriad vessels, while on it might ride in
safety all the navies of the world.

It was a fit theme for a picture, — the group of
rough trampers of the forest around that liquid
jewel, dipping from its tiny cup, and the magnificent city of Manhattan queening it over the broad

waters, with the thousand barks that ride upon their rolling billows.

Refreshed by the tea (fittest of all beverages for the woods), we rose, and began the descent (corresponding to the ascent) of the Pass. Now bending low beneath some arch-like crag, now squeezing through some ragged fissure, we urged our way. We passed a pyramid of gray rock, very peculiar; and descending rapidly, the magnificent wall of the Indian Pass was swallowed in the forest. It sank suddenly, like a ship at sea.

Standing on the floor of the gorge we were, as observed, eighteen hundred feet above tide. How grand, how lofty, the scale of Nature on every hand. Eighteen hundred feet above the sea, and the Pass rearing its fearful rampart fifteen hundred more, dizzily into the heavens.

Again the twining woods; one mile achieved, woods; two miles, woods; three, woods; four, woods! But now they break away; a wild green hill-side is in front, where the rich bee-hives of the blackberry and the red turbans of the raspberry are seen in profusion. We allow a handful or two of the luscious beauties to melt on the lap of the tongue, then onward. Frequent corduroys ribbing the loose quaking grass occur; rough fields succeed, with the sweet, kindly music of the cow-bell smiting the ear, and telling that man was not far distant. Blocks of old cord-wood, black with the weather, stand either side the way, which has widened into a rough cart-track, with corduroys as before. Another mile, and the green, pretty street of the Upper Works, with one brown meandering footpath in its midst, filled our eye a little distance in front. A cattle-picture, formed by the herd of Hunter, the sole resident with his family of the hamlet, showed itself before one of the low buildings on our right, while a mare and colt grazed the grassy margin of the street, which stretched " green to the very doors " in a southerly direction. It was a sweet, peaceful, rural scene in the red evening glow, and in beautiful contrast to the stern forest we for the present had left.

The abandoned village of the Upper Works occupies a plateau or high valley in the grand mountains whose tops break up the sky all around it ; although not one, not even Wallface, McIntyre, or Mount Robertson, whose breaths are constantly felt there, is visible from the village.

With glad footsteps we descended into this little Auburn of the woods, passing the ruins of " the Forge," and restricting ourselves to the home path, the delicious green sward either way looking as if wheel had never scarred its beauty. While within the Indian Pass, I became aware of a lameness, threatening to be serious, in my right foot, which on examination I found proceeded from a deep chafe (the very thing I was apprehensive of before starting) of the copper of my shoe on my instep. An incipient limp, as I passed along, warned me to make head-quarters in the hamlet, for a few days at all events, to restore my foot to its original soundness and usefulness, ere trying the rugged ascent of Tahawus.

With this view we stopped at Mr. Hunter's, and I proceeded to make myself comfortable. I soon formed an acquaintance with Hunter himself, an intelligent Scotchman, and his kind family; and shortly we had tea around his hospitable board. I then sauntered without.

The cattle-picture had become locomotive, each member picturesquing on his own hoof, as well as "hook;" but the colt still grazed by its dam, as if not caring for all the cattle-groupings in the hamlet. The low light streamed down the grassy street tinging it into gold-velvet. Hunter's superb rooster, his plumage one opal, reared his lordly crest and strutted by his "feathered dames," and a splendid drake waddled by the side of his mate, his gemmy shape all aglow. The cattle-picture was now restored at the foot of the village, toward Lake Sanford; and away over the level fields leading to Lakes Sallie and Jamie or Hamish, the stumps began to shimmer in the transparent dark. At the door, one of Hunter's bright-eyed children was feeding an eager calf from a bucket. The animal, in spite of the thrustings back of the boy, insisted on burying his head and shoulders in the bucket, as if feeling the last pangs of hunger, his tail all the while swinging like the tongue of a bell. The child at last thrust the animal entirely back. He looked up amazed, wheeled his tongue into the corners of his mouth, made another dive for the bucket, missed it, and then went contentedly to grazing.

At this, the colt looked up with its bright intelligent eye, lifted its tail like a musket, stamped, and whinnied as if in inquiry. The dam ceased her croppings, and giving a side blow, like a box on the ear, to her young, stooped again to her supper; while the young colt, receiving " more kicks than coppers,"and with curiosity entirely satisfied, bit a fly from its flank, cut a caper, and crouched down.

Up the green street went the cattle-groupings, they having turned at the end of the large boarding-house, that, with its score of eyes, seemed as intact as when the forge furnace blew its sunset steam-whistle signal for the hands to leave off work. On went the cattle, weaving as they went a series of pictures worthy of Cuyp, with the fine light of the last sunset gleaming upon them.

On each side stood the houses, so perfect, except

here and there a broken pane, I almost saw the people at the windows, or on the porches. One week of repairing would make them comfortable dwellings again, as they were a score of years ago.

I pictured to myself the usual evening scene of twenty years since, when the gladdening steam-whistle or joyful bell told the release of the work-people of both sexes, and they thronged the broad, grassy street, returning to their cosy homes; when the "Blast Furnace," now so still and solitary, poured out its denizens at the signal; when the whir of wheels no longer filled the air, nor the clang of machinery, the smite of hammers, nor the hum of work; and labor ceased for a while its efforts. But the scene changed. The distance from market, the badness of the roads, and expense of manufacturing the magnetic iron ore in this extremely lonely and remote region, buried in endless forests, checked the eager spirit of enterprise; and the unfortunate death of Mr. Henderson, the most active and influential partner in the business, completed the matter. The business was entirely abandoned, and from the day the last billet was cast into the furnace to the present, no whir of wheel, no hum of labor has been heard in the hamlet, nor will until some railroad opens with its creative, life-giving track this tremendous wilderness.

And now inexhaustible beds of magnetic iron ore, as large probably as any in the world, and fabulously rich, even to the extent of seventy or eighty per cent. of pure iron, slumber here or wait "for the good time coming." The very soil glitters with its crumbled particles. Its silver sparks flash from the pebbles on which you tread ; it crops out in every direction — in the bed of the brook, in the wreath of fern, in the fields you cross, and in the grass of the very street on which stands the village. The Hudson itself pours over an iron dam, and ripples down iron rocks.

The dam is another wonder of this wonderful region. Having heard of its existence, I accompanied Mr. Hunter one morning to examine it. Passing a little distance up the street, we turned into a rough stony pasture, through which the Hudson wound its way. Shortly a rumble was heard, and pausing at a barrier of black rock, over which the waters dashed, Hunter ejaculated " The Dam!" It extended completely across the channel, one smooth, sloping ledge or wall, with the glassy current almost like a film of isinglass sliding over, fringed with foam at the foot. We stepped across ankle-deep, and recrossed. Blocks of ore lay in the river above and below, the heedless water chafing and murmuring over and through them, blocks more precious than pearls or rubies, while the dam, of which the Hudson complained, in rumbling tones, for bridling his course, was richer than the bridge of gold leading to the Scandinavian Valhalla, theme of song for untold ages. Harp of poet has never sung of this at present simple barrier to a forest stream; but Aladdin's lamp never held more magic than it and its kindred rocks, nor the oriental ointment that changed deserts into cities, never worked more wizard wonders, than will this hidden wealth when Enterprise smites the rock with his wand, and opens, with his golden lily, the charmed portals of the forest-temple.

This magnificent deposit equals fully in richness, extent, and value, the Iron Mountain of Missouri, is easily worked, and can produce a steel equal to the best Russian and Swedish ores. It was first made known to the original proprietors, Archibald McIntyre, David Henderson, his son-in-law, and Duncan McMartin, by old Sabele, an Indian who haunted the region like an otter, long after his tribe had vanished.

" Me take you to a dam like beaver-dam, all black and shiny, where de water goes pom, pom, pom, for quart o' whiskey ! " was the salutation of the old fellow to one of the partners, accidentally in the region, as the Indian was setting a mink-trap in the Indian Pass ; and he was as good as his word.

A silver mine exists between Wallface and the Ausable River, a few miles from Scott's, but where, is, unfortunately, not known. The father of the present Mr. Scott, in hunting, became lost. In a large ledge adjoining his evening camp, the rich metal glittered on his rapt eye, but he was never able, after leaving the spot in the confusion of intellect to which all persons are subject who are lost in the woods, to identify it ; and to this day, guarded only by the grim " Genius loci," sleeps unknown this Potosi of the Adirondacks.

But superior in value to all the gold, silver, and diamond mines on earth, are the rich iron mines of the Upper Hudson. At some future time, Industry will again waken them, and give them once more to the world of man. It is incredible how the whole region is permeated with the ore. I have picked its heavy black blocks, lying loose on the remote shores of Lake Avalanche; with the print of the panther's foot fresh beside them, and have encountered them along the rocky " Flume " of the Opalescent River born in the mountain-meadow on the northeastern slope of Mount Marcy.

As I retrod the street of the hamlet on our return, I fancied I was treading on the buried city of Uhländ, that would rise to the jangling bell of the locomotive, and fill the spot with roofs, domes, and steeples. The ore glitters in the sunken hoof-track

of the wandering kine; it is unearthed by the tooth
of the grazing colt, or the nibble of the partlet; it
pervades the air from the grinding of the passing
wheel, and sparkles in the water you drink. It
strengthens the tall frame of Hunter, enters into
the system of his kindly wife, and glows in the
cheeks of his pretty daughters. I believe it even
entered my frame during my three days' sojourn,
thus enabling me to encounter, without flinching,
the terrors of old Tahawus. At all events, I think
it entered into my great toe, for it became marvel-
ously strong in a very short time.

Sunset melts, twilight deepens, the moon rises.
The cattle picture is cut in silver before the boarding-house, and the whole village dreams in the
seraphic light. From the low hills west toward the
Preston Ponds comes the wail of some night bird,
and hark! the voice of Hunter's wakeful chanticleer,
mistaking, probably, the bright light for daybreak,
rings like a gun-fire through the hamlet. On the
air sounds the steady rumble of the Iron Dam, and
bidding adieu for the present to moonlight and
musings, I seek my little cosy room in Hunter's
dwelling and am soon in the "Land of Nod."

"Cock-a-doodle-doo!" Over the village it rings
like a reveille, followed by "quack, quack!" like
"taps." I rise, dress quickly, and sally out. Dawn
is brightening over the hamlet. The cattle are mak-

ing another Paul Potter picture in the street by the
well-sweep. Half a dozen are standing in picto-
rial attitudes. One has just risen from the silver-
frosted ground, peeling a delicate sheet of pearl
from the grass; one stands with its neck stretched,
lowing; one is looking, with mad eye and lowered
brow, at a little curly pet of a dog belonging to the
family, while one of the daughters of Hunter has
just taken the red pail to milk old Crumple in the
crispy field. Hark! a loud boom! Has the Iron
Dam severed itself from the river, and taken to
flying, "like Loretto's Chapel," through the air?
Why, no! it is only a bumble-bee! Boo-m-m-m-m!
It will waken all the echoes in the village! Me-
thinks this very butterfly, wavering along, hums in
his smooth, velvet flight! Hark! a tremendous
sound this time! a galloping — a rising dust! Halloo! what on earth is here! — a charge of cavalry, or rather calvesalry, from the hill-side, through
the openings between the houses down the street of
the village! The three calves have let themselves
loose, and are charging with sabres, or rather, tails,
in air, full tilt upon us! How the trumpets or, not
to put too fine a point upon it, their ba-ba's sound.
Mercy! what shall we do! But lo! an opposing
charge by the colt *solus*, full gallop against the
coming foe! The parties meet midway, the colt's
heels flourishing like a couple of carbines. I am

sorry to say, the calves show the white feather and their white tails at the same time, flourishing, in turn, a swift dozen of heels in ignoble flight up the street, towards Lake Henderson. And this reminds me, — I must visit Lake Henderson.

Accordingly, I follow the fierce dragoons up the street, and ascending, to the left, a steep wood-road to where Mount Robertson heaves grandly upward, at length descend to an arm of the lovely lake, glittering in the varied foliage. Here I find a dug-out moored among the lilies, and, seizing the paddle, I soon float into the midst of the lovely mirror. At my left, soars the splendid flank of Robertson, one smooth slope of leaves. A little north and looking over its shoulder, peer the summits of Mount Henderson, farther toward the "Mountain of the White Star." In front, far above the intervening forest, due north, towers the curved bastion of the Indian Pass, brought so near by my opera-glass that I see the cracks and crevices of its gray surface. It sits so high above the rest of the scene, showing from base to brow, it seems as if it might detach itself, and move majestically down upon the lake. This grand lift of the Pass, shows vividly the height which must be attained before even reaching its sublime portal. There the rocky wall stood, as if propping the very heavens! Opposite, frowned the wild breast of Mount Mc-

Intyre, which, although twice the altitude of the
Pass, from its gradual slope, looked not nearly
so lofty. On my right, over a ridge, rose the dark
cone of Mount Colden (formerly Mount McMartin), with a jagged edge running from its crest
toward its base, the north profile of the great Trap
Dike, — as I afterwards discovered, cutting through
the entire front of the stern mountain, where it
looked toward Lake Avalanche. But, as I saw it
then, I fancied it the profile of the guardian
spirit of the region, gazing grimly at the gradual
encroachments of man on his dominions.

The afternoon light was glowing softly on the
waveless water, yielding it a tinge the warm color
of claret, and the dragon-flies were flashing through
the rushes, while that beautiful torment, the black
fly (it is a mistake that it perishes in July, it lives
until the strong frost comes), with a play of gold
on its glossy wings, and bronze tints flitting over its
sable shape, lighted on my flesh and nipped with
its little pincers. And the wood-duck, " atom of
the rainbow," skimmed along, kindling the water
as it went. I floated to the southern bank, where
shone the stream that links the lake to Lake Harkness farther south, and, after an hour of sylvan silence and solitude, and running a severe race with
a scared water-rat, I left the lake and returned to
the village.

4

Mars, Alexander, Cæsar, and Napoleon! a field-day is in progress. The three calves are drawn up in dragoon order, led by the colt. The ducks are grouped in the centre, and the cattle, one solid body like the Greek phalanx, follow. The whole array are passing in review before Colonel Chanticleer, who is standing on one leg in all his bravery by the well-sweep. The dame partlets of his family are clustered behind, admiring his grand movements.

It was really majestic to see the Colonel, with his head curved high to the imminent dislocation of his neck, his proud eyes staring at the advancing host, and his rainbow tail curled magnificently as he awaited the coming of the martial column.

A crow from his stretched throat, with a pre-liminary flap of his stately wings, announced the near approach of the mighty array, as the trumpet announced the march of the Roman legion.

On trampled the cavalry, headed by Lieut.-Colonel Colt, on tramped the infantry; the ducks flaunted their colors; and the curly pup which popped from the house, at this opportune moment, let stream a volley of music. This lasted some little time; the review then ceased, and the regiment was dismissed. I am sorry to say that the music, at this time, began a series of capers like a crazy drum-major. He seized Lieut.-Colonel

Colt by the tail, who launched out in the most undignified manner, but fortunately without hitting the little Arab. This magnificent Pasha with one tail, however, came within an ace, or rather a bite, of not having any, for Music, with a spiteful snap, nearly severed it in twain. It ended with his Worship dangling two tails, for the bite had the effect of making it lop down with an angle that added not a little to the worshipful Pasha's dignity. He was of a contrary opinion, however, for he tucked it between his legs in the most sneaking style, and went to grazing by his dam — the very picture of disconsolateness. Next, pup scuttled after the ducks, that lowered their colors and waddled off, quacking as if they smelt the gridiron. Lastly, the little marauder flew at Colonel Chanticleer, who, to his shame be it spoken, showed not only the white feather, but all his feathers, in scrambling off before his family, which were cackling a dirge to his dishonor, and only found refuge on the fence, where Music stopped, grinned, gaped, and stalked away with an air of triumph. The Colonel finding himself safe, flapped his wings, crowed, and seeing that Music had departed, flew back to his family, lifted one leg again, and robbed a hen of a seed which she had just scratched from the soil.

Quiet settled down once more on the hamlet. The houses seemed so fast asleep, that I thought in the glimmering light they nodded.

Down the low hills at the west, walling in (also on the north) the village, the sunshine streamed, making yellow vistas between the buildings, and spreading pleasantly over the grass in front, so as to fill the street with golden richness. A glitter danced upon the colt; a duck showed a play of colors; and a partlet seemed as full of hues as a deer-fly.

These hills had been partially cleared into rough lots, but the forest still crowned them, and reached half-way down their sides.

East, over the wild fields where the Adirondack River ran toward (and into) Lake Sanford, frowned the wilderness in the direction of Tahawus, scattered with the early Autumn hues, and with outpost trees, rich in red and golden tints.

I looked around and enjoyed my situation in this little village, sixteen miles of forest separating it one way from the Elizabethtown Road, five and a half miles another, from any settlement, and over a broken corduroy that sets the teeth chattering at the very mention, — thirty miles another, from the Keene settlements, and fifteen miles another, from the Racket waters that, in turn, are away from everybody (almost).

The cloudless sun was still two hours high, and the September day smiled so soft, sweet, and genial, that I determined to visit Lake Sanford, lying

south of the village. I took the " Blast Furnace "
on the way, going through it from bottom to top.
It stands at the side of the road, on a sunny knoll,
the brow of which is level with the attic of the
building, so that the little iron fire-engine could be
run from the garret directly on to the summit, and
thence to the spot where it was needed. Everything appertaining to the Furnace was in " apple-
pie " order, thanks to the ceaseless care of Hunter,
who acted as agent of the Company, the now owners
of the property,—they having purchased it from the
heirs of the original proprietors. The gutta-percha
pipes, wheel-bands, and other appurtenances were
preserved entire. I glanced into a dark receptacle
of enormous wheels, a perfect entanglement — now
motionless, and thought of the whirling and thundering once prevailing there. In the room above
I saw the furnace, a splendid structure of brick
and cut granite, built as if for ages, and in perfect
preservation; everything about looking, in fact, as
if but recently abandoned. The black iron dust
was still mounded in spots, and the long, massive
iron rake used to rake out the furnace, was lying,
as if dropped yesterday, and seemingly waiting
to be again lifted by the brawny arms that would
probably know it no more. The quiet sunshine
looked in through the chinks and knot-holes, gilding the iron-work and checkering the whole broad

room. Not even a rat appeared to have disturbed
the order and silence of the deserted spot. To have
heard even the gnaw of the little carpenter would
have been welcome as giving signs of life.

A score of rods brought us (Merrill and Robert,
my two faithful guides, had accompanied me) to the
outlet of Lake Sanford, which stretches its liquid
arm to the Lower Works. We found a leaky
scow half-way up the sandy bank, with a pair of
oars, and embarked. We passed a small island
midway the channel, and presently opened upon
the lake. Its waters appeared equally divided by
a large island, reflecting the soft white clouds and

"The (autumn) heaven's delicious blue."

We rowed some distance down the lake and
turned. The east sky-line was broken up by ragged tops of enormous mountains, among which old
Tahawus, the Dial, and Dix's Peak were the most
conspicuous. We blended our voices for a response
from Echo Mountain, swelling boldly from the lake.
The echo bounded out like the blast of a thousand
trumpets. Again, again, and again the wizard voice
repeated our shout, — each time softer, sweeter,
softer, fainter, sweeter, fainter, far away, away-
way, as if magic music was melting o'er the
water —

"The horns from Elf-land faintly blowing!"

now the shadow, now the flitting transparency of

sound, until all died away into stillness, wafting our very breath away with it.

Regaining the outlet, I glanced up, and lo! the Indian Pass in its splendid half-circle, seemingly as near as at Lake Henderson, and, like Mount Morris at Big Tupper's Lake, omnipresent except at the village. The hated sounds of man probably induced the old monster to shroud himself from gaze there in sublime disgust. Opposite also appeared the wooded capes of Mount McIntyre. Mooring our bark once more upon the bank, we returned to the village.

Sunset came in golden-gray, lovelier than the last. The cattle scattered again their panoramic pictures along the street; the Pasha of two tails grazed by the side of its dam, both striking attitudes of their own. The geese, with a sudden clamor and clapping of wings, fluttered a short distance, then dropped, each depositing their pinions, one above the other, by their sides, and waddled in single file, as if in caricature of the stately review lately enacted, to their rest; while Colonel Chanticleer, at the head of his particular squad (who ever saw a colonel without his aids), strutted along, lifting one foot after another as if the ground was hot, — keeping a bright lookout, however, for Music, who was fortunately absent. At length the Colonel led his aids to the roosting-place at

the side of the house. I watched the way the
band roosted. Each hen, with a hoarse scream, as
if horror-struck at her own temerity, flew up to
the pole. The great Colonel, standing erect below,
alternately looked and winked (always keeping an
eye out for the dreaded appearance of Music) until,
with one bold flap, he himself sought the roost in his
overwhelming majesty, and gave one bold clarion-
crow — nipped short, however, by Music, who appeared at this moment as if to resent this encroachment upon his tuneful privileges. Secure from
harm, the Colonel then looked with "bended bow"
(beak I mean) mute disdain upon Music, and settled himself for the night, slowly, magisterially
"folding the drapery" of his feathers "around
him," and casting one magnificent glance over his
clinging aids.

CHAPTER III.

MOUNT MARCY.

Departure from the Upper Works. — The Monument. — Lake Colden. — Lake Avalanche. — The Shower.

THE next morning, my foot being healed, thanks to the magic ointment of kind Mrs. Hunter and the yellow plasters of a very nice, friendly young Philadelphian who, with his little bright-eyed brothers, was passing the summer at the village, shooting partridges around lakes Sallie and Jamie, I concluded to start for Tahawus, fifteen miles distant. Again I donned the copper shoe, and, with my guides and Hunter to set us on the trail to the old mountain, left the latter's worthy family with warm regret, hoping, at some future time, again to see them.

We passed with rapid pace through this little Petra of the desert, and at its head, I turned aside with Hunter up a steep ascent, to take a farewell look at Mount Robertson. On the brow of the acclivity I paused, transfixed in admiration. There swelled the magnificent mountain, spotted

with rich hues and leaning on the soft autumn
sky, with a bright streak at its foot, like a weather-
gleam on the sky's rim, telling of Lake Henderson.
Beyond, a sea of forest rolled, weltering, around
Santanoni and Mount Henderson, surging up and
over Mount Seward, billowing about the wild Preston Ponds and Cold River tangled in the woods
like a silver thread.

" How many mountains are there around the
Upper Works? " I asked.

" There's Wallface, McIntyre, Mount Robertson, Santanoni, Henderson, Mount Seward, Colden, Marcy, Haystack, Blue Mountain, Dix's Peak,
the Dial, Boreas Mountains, and Ausable Mountains, and not one seen from the village," answered
Hunter, leading the way back to my companions.
How like the mountains of his future life to the
youth in his native hamlet, thought I.

Rejoining my guides, and saying good-by to my
good friend Hunter, the very soul of kindness,
Merrill, Robert, and I crossed the splendid Iron
Dam (mine of pearls, rubies, diamonds, emeralds,
sapphires, gold, and silver to future ages), and, leaving behind us a wild clearing or two and a wild
meadow, — the long beaver grass swaying to our
progress, — we entered the forest. How grateful
the plunge into its cool shadow from the beating
sun-glow without! It was like the emerald wings

of Thalaba's bird between him and the burning-
glass heat of the desert. How I reveled, too, in
the elastic feel of the springy soil under my steps!
And the air, how pungent and fragrant! I recognized a dozen mingling perfumes, — the balsamic
scent of the pine, the wild odor of the cedar, the
rich flavor of the juniper and sassafras, and the delightful perfume of the ripening herbage. Onward
led the narrow trail, a mere touching streak, a
simple thread amid the bewildering labyrinth of
trees. On, on! now dipping into the green hollow
of the pebbly brook, now ascending the hill of hemlocks, twining now around the swamp and edging
the ravine; past "Indian doors" (saplings bent into
bows by others weightier), — on, still on! Miles
melted. Through gloom and glow, over dingle and
glade pleasant and sweet, enjoying the brief, delicious rests on the plump cushion of the mossy root,
then up once more, and away, — on, still on. At
last an opening glimpsed among the trees at our
left, and we emerged into a beaver-meadow, with a
small pond glittering, like a dropped gem, in a corner. But what instantly arrested our attention, so
strange, did it seem in this wild, remote spot, was
a beautiful monument of Nova Scotia freestone, —
its light chocolate hue somewhat weather-tinged —
which color, however, had imparted to it a more
mellow appearance. It was finished in the highest

art, and carved with the readiest skill, and stood on a rock opposite the pond, and near the edge of the wood toward Lake Colden. It was the monument " erected by filial affection," thus ran the touching inscription, " to the memory of our dear father David Henderson, who accidentally lost his life on this spot, 3d September, 1845." It was a short, simple, square column, with a sculptured ornament or capital on the top, a wreath at the upper edge, and another ornament on the upper face of the column with the inscription below. A bass-relief was sculptured immediately beneath an urn, with an anchor, emblem of Hope, placed perpendicularly athwart a Bible opened diagonally. The emblems still showed as sharply cut as when first carved, and were entire, excepting a fluke of the anchor, accidentally (let us hope) broken.

Mr. Henderson was exploring the woods around the Upper Works, then in full operation, with the famous hunter, John Cheny (immortalized by that fine poet and noble gentleman, Charles Fenno Hoffman, one of the brightest stars that ever glittered in the intellectual sky of New York, his native State), accompanied by his little son, ten years of age. John had gone to the pond, and Mr. Henderson was resting on the rock. A pistol-shot echoes. Henderson falls, and, in a few moments after ·he was reached by the horror-stricken Cheny, he expires, with an invocation to his son to be a good boy, and take care of his bereaved mother.

" To die ! " moaned the unfortunate gentleman, " and in such a spot! " a few moments before he breathed his last. He had laid his pistol on the rock, — the sudden contact brought down its hammer, — it exploded, and sent its fatal bullet into the heart of its owner.

With praiseworthy care, his loving children reared this beautiful memento to his cherished memory, in this wild meadow, at the base of grand Mount McIntyre (named in honor of his father-in-law), which towers in leafy solitude at the north, and encircled by the tangled wilderness.

The monument was cut and carved abroad, and, in separate pieces, was transported on the backs of Hunter and several of the workmen of the Upper Works, to the rock, and there erected.

How often has the wild wolf made his lair beside it ! how often the savage panther glared at its beautiful proportions, and wondered what object met his blazing eyeballs !

After a brief rest in a mossy hollow and partaking a hasty meal, again I started, preceded by my guides. How swift the minutes glide in these forest-rests, and so, indeed, do the minutes of life glide away! And yet how important are they, and of what momentous interests ! As the Mohammed-

an never casts away the least scrap of paper, lest
the name of God should be written on it, so should
our minutes be cherished, as they may bear characters affecting our dearest interests, both in Time
and Eternity!

All the roughness of the forest appeared concen-
trated between Calamity Pond (named from the
disaster) and Lake Colden, as evil fortunes are
sometimes clustered on our way in life. The trail
crossed a perfect chopping sea of ridges, tasking
our energies more than any preceding day.

Sunset was smiling when we reached the little
hunter's shanty near Lake Colden. The latter,
however, was hidden by a screen of forest. Below, the outlet crept on toward its intersection with
the east branch of the Hudson, the Opalescent
River mingling its faint murmurs with the fainter
twitterings of the woods.

My guides deposited their knapsacks in the
shanty, and in a few minutes, we all stood on the
margin of the beautiful lake. Aye beautiful, truly
beautiful! A rosy light trembled on the water,
which reflected in transparent shadow the bare,
savage cliff of Mount Colden on our right, and the
rich woods of Mount McIntyre opposite, with a
low, leafy ridge at the north.

Thus three shadows rested on the lake, leaving
clear only the heart. The engraving in the Geo-

logical Reports, and in Headley's charming volume,
" The Adirondack," gives a most perfect idea of the
singular appearance of the lake from these shadows.
And here, also, I wish to bear testimony to the
graphic accuracy of the engraving of the loftiest
point of the Indian Pass, in the same graphic book
of Mr. Headley. It is a perfect photograph of the
magnificent sight, in consonance with the vivid
word-paintings of the celebrated author.

I sat down on a low, black log, fringed with
waterplants, to study the enchanting sunset picture,
while my guides visited a wooded point below, for
the purpose of building a cedar raft to waft us
over the lake toward Lake Avalanche in the
morning. A rich flush bathed the terrific precipices and filled the wild gorges of Mount Colden
(the most savage mountain, by far, of the Adirondacks, — the very wild-cat of mountains). And
the lake! how bewitching in its loveliness. It was
the Sleeping Beauty of the Enchanted Forest,
watched over by frowning giants. A duck was lav-
ing his jeweled hues in the blush-rose radiance, and
the jet head of a water-rat, like a skimming tur-
quoise, dotted the exquisite sheet in one of its fairy
coves. How lovely, how lovely the scene! here,
out in the wilderness alone, repeating its tale of
beauty, sunset after sunset, to naught but the moun-
tain-woods.

A sweet silence reigned, broken only by the few notes of the birds, bidding good-by to the scene, and the click of the axe and careless laugh of the two woodmen framing their raft in the neighboring cove.

In a short time rose a hubbub from the point, and the raft appeared, propelled by the planted poles of the guides, and ruffling up the rich enamel of the water. For a rod, the thing floated well enough, but in a few minutes, it struck and clung upon a small island of grass, and the guides waded ashore. This little incident over, the scene resumed its holy peace. Nothing now but the low silver chirping of the mountain-finch settling into rest, awoke the slumbering air. The pine soared up, "still as a mouse," — even the aspen slept. It was —

"Silence slumbering on her instrument."

Determined on seeing the scene steeped in the silver of the bonnie moon, I now left with my guides for the shanty and our supper.

At midnight we started for the lake. We crossed the outlet, and soon the moonlight painting of Colden was gleaming before us. A path of shifting meteor brilliance shivered on the water, while the glossy shadows thrown by Mounts McIntyre and Colden, were more sharply defined by the contrast. A small black space in the shallows, denoted the raft. A serene quiet brooded over the silver scene;

as if the naiad of the lake was sleeping, after touching her harp to the Dolphin glories of the dying day. An inexpressible feeling of solitude and silence weighed over the whole scene. I seemed an intruder on its beauteous slumber, stretched, as it were, in the delicate sheen of the lovely moon and black velvet of the mountain shadows. Blazing in the beauty of the dainty light — the daintiest of lights! how few, I thought, of earth's denizens awake as they might be to every sensation, knew that here, in the core of the savage wilderness, glowed a sight to awaken their deepest enthusiasm, their loftiest ideal of beauty! The ripples murmured their fairy music, the pearly light sparkled in the murmuring ripples, the lake's heart glittered, and I sat entranced. That glittering water! It was hope when life was dark; love, when the heart was forsaken; friendship, when our path was lonely.

After photographing the scene on my memory, I returned with my guides to the shanty. I lay on my couch of spruce and mused. How rough and difficult had my path proved from my point of departure to the present, and such a radiant close! It was a rich sunset after a rainy day, joy after much sorrow.

And yet how my sinews had been braced by my exertions and fatigues. Is not the rough path of

5

life the best? Most indubitably! Do not its roses enervate and finally destroy? Most indubitably also. As Hannibal's soldiers, after triumphing over the frozen Alps, were vanquished by the luxuries of Capua, so has many a strong spirit, after its victories over adverse fate, been conquered by the prosperity it wearied every energy to obtain.

The following day was devoted to Lake Avalanche. None but one or two of the state geologists had, as far as I could ascertain, ever penetrated to this extremely remote water. And our desire to visit it was intensified at the thought. We, therefore, as the rubies and topazes of the fresh light were gleaming around us, left our shanty breathing like a dewy rose in the morning air, and the red spangle of our camp-fire to blink itself down into ashes, while we essayed the unbroken solitude of the way to the savage lake.

The raft was moored still at the isle of water-plants owned by King Muskrat, and a few minutes' exertion, on the part of Merrill and Robert, brought it to where I could embark. My guides bent to their poles, and we rippled a little way into the lake, when another shallow caught our platform, and we left it to its fate, ourselves wading ashore.

We then essayed our only other practicable way, the side of Mount Colden, for a glance at the steep shores of Mount McIntyre, plunging almost sheer

into the water, convinced us it was folly to try
our fortune there. There was no trail to guide us,
and we struck boldly on to break our way athwart
this most wild and savage mountain. Had I known
the difficulties I was about to encounter, I should, I
think, have attempted to swim Lake Colden rather
than have dared the horrors of that tramp — that
positively frightful journey across the flank of the
almost precipitous summit — one chaos of prostrate
trees and woven boughs. I shudder now, when I
think of its fatigues and its dangers.

An enormous mass of high, wide drift, composed
of tough tree-tops heaped by some ancient hurricane
— a perfect *chevaux de frise* — presented its sharp
tangle of points nearest the lake-shore, and, finding
it impervious, we were forced to strike farther up
the side of Mount Colden. It was scarcely mend-
ing the matter, for a terrific wind here had, years
ago, dashed the trees into a twisted labyrinth of
fallen stems and branches, mantled with moss cer-
tainly six feet thick. There was no trail, as I said,
so we were obliged to pick our own way. Soon we
came to a line of fresh panther-tracks (deep, huge,
showing the enormous size of the creature), which
we gladly followed. How significant that circumstance of the utter wildness of our way, the almost
absolute certainty of our being the first for many,
many years, to attempt the visit of this most re-

cluse, untamed, and almost unknown lake. No
other way across the mountain was practicable,
except possibly the summit, shown by the fact that
our trail was solely followed by two or three other
parties visiting the lake that season, after ourselves.
How toilsome and dangerous was that journey!
Not knowing where to plant my steps, my guides
being in front, in some instances I broke through
the brittle moss to my knees, waist, and even
arm-pits. Once I fell into an unknown depth,
only saved from falling farther by clinging to a
branch! Great, fallen trunks also interposed their
ramparts; limbs wreathed around me like serpents. Sometimes the trunks crumbled at the
touch of my mounting foot, letting me into their
damp ruins, slimy as the skin of a black-snake.
Sharp rocks, concealed under the treacherous moss,
thrust their fangs into my feet and mangled my
flesh, until I almost screamed with the agony.
Below, I caught glimpses of quiet Lake Colden, as
if it rejoiced at my trouble in daring thus to in-
trude into its sylvan and lovely domain. However,
everything comes to an end at last, and so did my
journey, by our reaching the ridge between us and
Lake Avalanche. Our level path leading through
tall herbage, was soon trod, and wading through a
few bushes, we ascended a small acclivity, and the
deep, black waters of Avalanche were before us.

Almost the counterpart of Lake Colden, it equals the latter in beauty, or rather it owns all the soft loveliness of the latter, mingled with a wildness the other wears not. The precipices of Mount Colden are here more terrific, and the wooded grandeur of Mount McIntyre is more imposing, while the outline of the ridge at the north of Avalanche, is more jagged and sawlike. Lake Colden shows the beauty of the deer and Avalanche that of the catamount.

I made my way to a tall rock, emerald with moss and gray with lichen, on the immediate shore of the pure, transparent lake, and sat down to stamp the scene upon my heart. The ragged fracture of the great Trap Dyke, so famous among geologists, calling forth their warmest enthusiasm, and cut so deeply (one hundred feet) into the flinty ashy gray hypersthene of Mount Colden, frowned directly opposite. The mole that mined it, was a small spring gnawing the rocks, which were split above as well as below.

The deep waters, like ebony, with a glitter upon their black glass, lay below, and I thought how seldom they had been disturbed by human presence. Here, alone in the forest (I repeat the thought), quite removed from even extraordinary travel, lies the sable gem, with none to see its wondrous beauty. How patiently from hour to hour does it mirror the sky-tints and the wood-colors! How it has smiled to the sun, dimpled to the breeze, blackened to the storm since it heard the primal anthem.

And, as if in response to the blackening, suddenly the bright scene turned dim. A shower was upon us, — one of those generally lurking in the gorges of these mountains, like echoes, ready to roam out at the slightest provocation. The quick, bright drops began to tinkle on the lake like little bells. A glittering flashed out over the dark water to each pelt of the drops, which pelted me also like spent bullets. I was commencing to forget my wood-craft, and to feel annoyed. The whole scene was now streaked in the gray shower. A merry music burst out upon the lake, as if the lovely naiad of Avalanche was tuning her harp in unison with the glad pattering of the leaves. I was looking at the smooth, iron-like precipice opposite, when, suddenly, white tinges appeared to break from the surface. I rubbed my eyes! What were they? What on earth were they? Was a silver mine oozing from the stern, hard rock? There they shone — remnants, they seemed to my excited fancy, of the Angel of the Sunlight's white raiment as she floated away before the gathering shower.

It was only after riveting my gaze, that I became aware the sight was a multitude of fairy waterfalls, born of the rain, and foaming, through the innumerable and to me invisible wrinkles of the precipice, down to the lake. In some places, the minute streaks seemed like inlaid threads of silver, — the distance rendering them apparently motionless. In others, they were aggregated into a broad dazzling space like a pearly breastplate. Below, all the threads were united, and, owing to the greater roughness of the surface, they were seen in full motion, one expanse of sliding scallops, as if an invisible loom were at work there, weaving the beautiful shapes. These, in turn, were mingled into a basin whence, in one bold leap, a glittering curve sprang below, and, lost for a moment behind a screen of foliage, foamed forth and dashed with a pleasant rumble into the lake. The last of this fairy show was exhibited in a streak of white bubbles, that flashed slowly, and melting as they flashed, past my rock, and marched upward toward the head of the lake.

So beautiful was the whole display, — so in contrast with the frightful precipice, that I could only testify my admiration by exclamations. This silver frost-work, this magic picture was, of itself, sufficient to repay all my fatigue, and the hours passed in the wild solitude of my tramp. It seemed as if the shower had risen purposely to show me this lovely child of its cunning workmanship, its wizard sculpture, its fairy painting.

While I was thus admiring it, the transparent rain melted, the lake's song ceased; but still that pearly beauty shone against the rock, as if to prolong its life in pure triumph at the admiration it had caused. At last the delicate threads began to dwindle and break, spots vanished in the white breastplate like sparks in ashes, but still the loom poured out the graceful, shifting scallops, until the dark rock showed bare above them. Then they began to melt, although the crystal crescent of the leap still gleamed. At last the scallops died, the leap suddenly disappeared, the rumble below sounded a little longer, and then all was still. The picture and song were over. The streak of bubbles melted, and naught but glintings and sparklings in the woods, told the visit of the shower.

How warmly and genially the sun-glow broke upon us! Although we were three thousand feet above Lake Champlain, the warmth would have been a little oppressive, had not our bath somewhat chilled us, for autumn had mixed its breath a little with the rain, notwithstanding the almost unparalleled lingering of the summer, during my whole visit to the Adirondacks. So late an autumn was before rarely known, and I almost catch myself mingling my summer scenes of previous visits with this autumn one. Indeed, were it not for the hues, I should have forgotten it was not summer.

We sat and enjoyed the drying process, the sponging of the sunshine, until it was time to set out on our return. We recrossed the intervening ridge, and at sunset, after retracing our trail, without, however, the severe toil it cost to break it, arrived at our shanty, nearly breathless and heartily tired. After a frugal supper, I sat and watched the night brightening beneath the soaring moon. How inexpressibly lovely looked the moonlit woods! how still in the serene quiet of the watching heavens!

This dreamy light never seems so charming as when softening the stern grandeur of the forests. It silvers the rose, it sparkles on the dew, it streams on the glassy rill, it yields a more delicate grace to all rural Nature; but in the woods it is enchantment. How it kindles the dark waters of the lonely lake and bathes the beetling crags of the frowning mountain! Never had the beautiful orb looked so beautiful as once when I saw her beaming upon the terrific Clove of Whiteface, tinging the leap of the wild Ausable down the scowling chasm, fringed with rocks and pointed with tottering cedars. It was Purity smiling pityingly upon Sin; Innocence looking inquiringly upon Guilt.

> And art thou, Moon! akin to earth!
>   Is thine, like this, a suffering clime,
> Where hearts dwell prisoners from their birth,
>   And sighs to hurrying years keep time?

Or art thou formed of loftier mould?
　　Nearer to thee, my God, more bright!
Home of the wings of hovering gold,
　　Where Uriel stays his courier flight.

Art thou the clime of pastures green,
　　Of the still waters, Eden's own,
Roamed by the souls of statelier mien —
　　Those towering closest to the Throne?
Those waving high their boughs of palm,
　　And touching harps of sweetest sound;
Feeling the bliss of heavenly calm;
　　Treading the flowers of heavenly ground.

Vain thoughts! high, high o'er grief and tears,
　　High o'er the anguish of our lot,
Thou rollest through the rolling years;
　　On thy pure sheen no guilty blot!
Blent with the praising starry arch
　　O golden Moon! on, on thy course!
Proud joining the majestic march
　　Toward the grand God, of all the Source!

And I, an insect of a day,
　　Mote of a sunbeam, look on thee,
Drink the pure lustre of thy ray,
　　And think how blest with thee to be!
To dwell above this world of ours,
　　Forever freed, forever blest!
To gather wreaths of thornless flowers,
　　And quaff deep draughts of endless rest.

A pearly ray steeped a portion of the hemlock
couch piled in the shanty, and selecting this as the
nearest approach to the light of heaven, I was soon
asleep. All night did the outlet play its melodies

in my ear, mingling with my dreams. Now it
sounded a lute, now a trumpet.

> " And now 'twas like all instruments,
>   Now like a lonely flute,
>   And now it is an angel's song,
>   That makes the heavens be mute ! "

CHAPTER IV.

MOUNT MARCY.

On the Trail to Tahawus. — The Ascent. — Tahawus. — The Sunset. — The Sunrise. — The Panther Gorge. — Trail to the Ausable Ponds. — Moonlight Sail on the Upper Ausable.

LAKES Colden and Avalanche are linked by a stream, the outlet of the latter. Doubts had been expressed by those who had never visited Avalanche, whether the connecting stream was an outlet or inlet, — some even asserting that no stream existed. But we not only traversed its banks all the way to and from Lake Avalanche, but, to test the question of its direction, threw dead leaves into the current, which slowly, but very perceptibly, floated downward toward Lake Colden. And herein exists a singular fact. The bubbly streak of the Avalanche shower undoubtedly moved northward while the stream ran southward.

That the two lakes in the old time were one, cannot be denied. The ridge separating them was unquestionably formed by an enormous avalanche from the steep cliffs of Mount Colden. In fact,

avalanches are, even now, so common that the
Lake has thus received its picturesque name. And
what a slide to have smitten the one lake into
two! What thunders, as the mighty trees leaned
and tottered, and the rocks were hurled as from a
catapult, and the woods were rolled up, a mighty
billow, and the whole, a terrific cataract of mingled
trunks and crags, dashed into the lake, soaring into
two mighty walls, crowned with foam, and subsiding,
at last, into the present basins. It were worth a
life-time, almost, to have witnessed a sight so majestic.

A pine was sounding its low anthem to the sunrise as I awoke and prepared, with my guides, for
the labors of the day. They were to be the
most arduous of all, for they included the ascent
of Tahawus, the Sky-Piercer, known generally as
Mount Marcy. Tahawus, the Sky-Piercer! —
grand name for the soaring eagle of the stately
Adirondacks!

We crossed the outlet and struck the ascending
ground, immediately where the Opalescent River
(wildest of streams) linked the Colden outlet. A
fallen tree, bridging a foaming watercourse which
dashed into the Opalescent directly from the roots
of old Tahawus, led our steps across. Then up,
up, the fierce river brawling in its wide, glary,
rocky channel at our left. The closest woods were

twined around us, precluding sight save where, now
and then, the white of the Opalescent gleamed
through the breaks of the foliage. A mile thus
passed. At length we came to a wide opening
where the brawl of the stream was deepened into
a roar. Turning to the high banks, we saw
the mad torrent, dashing and foaming through a
narrow channel of rock splintered into pinnacles;
here plunging one sheet of spray within a basin
of bubbles, and there gushing, black and glossy,
through a throat-like passage, to be hurled down a
smooth declivity of granite. It was the famous
" Flume " of the Opalescent. For one mile did
the Flume continue with the same rush and roar,
among the pointed and splintered rocks. At length
the stream resumed its usual rapid but not cataract
character. Great blocks of gneiss stood here and
there in the channel through which the stream
dashed and curved, but it ran, generally, in a
straight direction. After vainly tempting the little
gemmed fairy trout of the wild stream at the numerous black basins bright with silver bubbles, we
resumed our customary pressing onward, with no
more pauses.

Dipping into hollows, straining up ridges, scrambling over logs, cleaving through moss treacherous
as alcohol, on, on we went. Here and there, we
crossed the Opalescent on its broken rocks, noticing

the manifold small fragments of iron ore, black and
massive and sparkling with bright sprinklings of the
ore, scattered in the channel. On past stars of fern
and brown twin-leafed sprouts of beech and maple ;
on past hopple-bush and crouching cedar ; on past
cloud-brushing pines, and hemlocks making net-work
of the blue ; on by oozing springs and lichen-crim-
soned boulders, still on, still on we went. My feet
moved up and down, instinctively, carrying my person without the slightest volition of will. Walking
had become a habit, and the frame conformed itself
to it. My whole system was thoroughly aroused,
so that quietude seemed unnatural. How glorious
was all that tramping of mine ! It was beatific !
toilsome, true, but productive of the most vivid delight. With what elastic feeling my feet bounded
from the leafen mould ! how like steel my sinews
performed their functions ! As the pearl hides in
the ocean and the gold in the mine, so is the
greatest physical enjoyment attainable only by the
most violent effort.

At length we came to a little green dell, bare
of trees, bordering the Opalescent, which we traversed a short distance. Then the trail suddenly
turned, leaving the river widely to the left. We
were probably a mile from its source, which lies, as
before stated, in a small meadow on the lofty flank
of Tahawus. This meadow is four thousand feet

above tide, and gives birth also to a branch of the West Ausable, flowing from the opposite rim at the north. The trail now became immediately steep, and Merrill suggested a lunch before proceeding farther. Although we supposed ourselves on the slope of Old Tahawus, neither of the guides, this visit being their first on this side, could indicate the fact with certainty. On wound the stealthy trail like a serpent, — on, on, through the close and to us, unknown woods.

With our cordial of tea glowing in my system, I again started, preceded by my guides. And now came the real tug! Up, up, up, without intermission! Drawing ourselves by pendent boughs, inserting our feet into fissures of the rocks, clutching wood-sprouts and knotted roots, and dangling by lithe saplings, up, up, up, with not a solitary level spot, we went, climbing thus our mountain-ladder. Loftier, as we went, rose the grand breast of an opposite mountain that we set down as Mount Colden. Up, up, up! the magnificent flank of Colden now heaving on high like an enormous ocean billow piled from hundreds of its fellows. It was awful, the sight of that mountain! its frown fairly chilled my blood. But up, up, still up. The trees that had hitherto towered into the sky, dwindled perceptibly, warning us that something was to happen. Up, up, still up.

Lower and lower the trees. Barer and barer the rocks. The noble pine of a quarter of an hour ago is now a sapling of a dozen feet. What will happen ? What dwarfing power broods above to cause this change ? But upward, upward still. Owing to the difficulties of the route, clinging to every object that presents, I cannot look upward! Steeper, if possible, the trail! See! the shrub I clutch, to drag myself ponderously upward, is the miniature pine whose stem, a short time since, would not crack ; no, although the angriest blast were hurled against it! What is to happen ? It was weird ; it was awful! A sensation of dread began crawling through my frame, something portentous and threatening to whisper hoarsely in my ear. What causes these haughty forests to bow their grand crests, and grovel upon the rocks ? WHAT ?

Up, up, still up! The shrub lies flat, a stiff verdant wreath, a mere crawling vine, a thing of wire, with scarce life sufficient to keep life! A chill breath too, commenced to permeate the air ; the breath of some monster whose lair was above. Be warned in time, O mortal, and approach no nearer ! Desolation and death frown before thee, and — ha! I chanced to look up ; and lo, a rocky dome, a dark pinnacle, an awful crest scowled above my head, apparently impending over it, as if to fall and crush me ; kept only by some invisible

6

agency from hurling itself downward upon my devoted person! WHAT WAS IT!

It was the stately brow of old Tahawus the Piercer of the Sky! Throned in eternal desolation, its look crushing down the soaring forest into shrubs, there it towered, the sublime King of the Adirondacks, its forehead furrowed by the assaults of a thousand centuries! There it towered, beating back the surges of a million tempests! There it stood, and — by Jove if there isn't a lizard crawling up there! or stop, let me see. Upon my modesty, if the lizard, by the aid of my glass, doesn't enlarge itself into Bob Blin! and there is Merrill following. And so I followed too. Showers of stones, loosened by my guides, rattled past. Still up I went. Over the precipitous rock by clambering its cracks and crannies, through its tortuous galleries, along the dizzy edges of the chasms. A score of times I thought the summit was just in front, but no; on still went my guides, and on still I followed. I began to think the nearer I approached the farther I was off. But at last Merrill and Robert both became stationary, in fact seated themselves, — their figures sharply relieved against the sky. Surmounting a steep acclivity, then turning into a sort of winding gallery, and passing a large mass of rock, I placed myself at their side, and lo, the summit! Famished with thirst, I looked around, and basins of water, hollowed in the stern granite, met my gaze, — real jewels of the skies, — rain water; and truly delicious was it. Next, my eye was sweetly startled by one of the most delicate little fairy flowers (a harebell) that ever grew — sweet as Titania, blue as heaven, and fragile as hope — here, on the very bald tip-top of old Tahawus. I looked around for humming-birds and butterflies! It was a beautiful sight, that little blossom trembling at the very breath, and yet flourishing here. Here, where the tawny grass sings sharp and keen in the wrathful hurricane that the eagle scarce dares to stem; where even the pine shrub cannot live, and the wiry juniper shows not even its iron wreath! Here, where the bitter cold lingers nearly all the year, and the snow-flake dazzles the June sun with its frozen glitter! Here, on the summit of a peak to which the lightning lowers its torch, and at whose base the storm cloud crouches.

A variety of mosses, several grasses, a species of dwarf creeping willow, and harebells, with other flowers of white and gold, spangle the mosses and seam the clefts of the summit.

And — what! a mellow hum in my ear! Is some fairy touching her tricksy harp among the flowers? It is from a honey-bee, by all that's wonderful! And see, a bumble-bee in its suit of black and gold! Swept upward on the broad pinions of the wind, they revel in the "hanging gardens" of blossoms that the old mountain offers.

The ascent of Tahawus is by no means an easy performance, an airy promenade. No! it is stern, persistent work; work that calls upon your mightiest energies! In attempting its ascent, strong, hardy trampers have given out, and lain down helpless in an attack of wood-sickness. And here is a new disease! I first heard of it in the Adirondacks! Wood-sickness! a sea-sickness on land! brought on by excessive fatigue, or by being buried, day after day, in the greenness of the woods — these tremendous, tangled, sun-concealing, weltering woods! The symptoms are the same as its sister of the sea; as disheartening and enfeebling.

Well here I am at last! I can hardly realize it! To tell the truth, I never thought I should ever reach the spot. Tahawus stood as a shining myth in my dreams — an abstraction — a formless form like the vision of Job — an image with an aureole — a something very grand and wild and sublime out in the woods, but which I never expected to see!

Clear and bright shines the prospect below, and herein we are lucky. Old Tahawus ofttimes acts sulky. He will not allow his vassal landscape to show itself, but shrouds it in a wet, clinging mist. To-day, however, he permits it to appear in his presence, and lo, the magic! A sea of mountain-tops! a sea frozen at its wildest tumult! And what a multitude of peaks! The whole horizon is full to repletion. As a guide said, " Where there wasn't a big peak, a little one was stuck up." Really true, and how savage! how wild! Close on my right rises Haystack, a truncated cone, — the top shaved apparently to a smooth level. To the west soars the sublime slope of Mount Colden, with McIntyre looking over its shoulder; a little above, point the purple peaks of Mount Seward — a grand Mountain Cathedral — with the tops of Mount Henderson and Santanoni in misty sapphire. At the southwest shimmers a dreamy summit, — Blue Mountain; while to the south stands the near and lesser top of Skylight. Beyond, at the southeast, wave the stern crests of the Boreas Mountain. Thence ascends the Dial,[1] with its leaning cone, like the Tower of Pisa; and close to it swells the majesty of Dix's Peak, shaped like a slumbering lion. Thence stagger the wild, savage, splintered tops of the Gothic Mountains at the Lower Ausable Pond, — a ragged thunder-cloud, — linking themselves, on the east, with the Noon-Mark[2] and Rogers' Mountain, that watch over the Valley of Keene. To the northeast rise the Edmunds' Pond summits — the mountain picture closed by the sharp crest of old Whiteface on the north — stately outpost of the Adirondacks. Scat-

---

[1] Called generally Nipple Top.
[2] Or Camel's Hump.

tered through this picture are manifold expanses of water — those almost indispensable eyes of a land-scape. That glitter at the. north by old Whiteface is Lake Placid; and the spangle, Bennett's Pond. Yon streak running south from Mount Seward, as if a silver vein had been opened in the stern mountain, is Long Lake ; and between it and our vision shine Lakes Henderson and Sanford, with the sparkles of Lake Harkness, and the twin lakes Jamie and Sallie. At the southwest glances beau-tiful Blue Mountain Lake, — name most suggestive and poetic. South, lies Boreas Pond, with its green beaver meadow and a mass of rock at the edge. To the southeast glisten the Upper and Lower Ausable Ponds; and farther off, in the same direction, Mud and Clear Ponds, by the Dial and Dix's Peak. But what is that long gleam at the east ! Lake Champlain ! and that glittering line north ! The St. Lawrence, above the dark sea of the Canadian woods.

I sat down to enjoy the scene, and make it an intaglio of my memory. A deep silence reigned. Then a whisper stole to my ear through the divine quiet, and I knew it was the mountain speaking to my heart.

" Vain mortal," these the words, " why this con-tinued disquiet ? Why dost thou wail in wretched-ness and darken in despair ? Why dost thou cloud thy little life with sorrows of thine own seeking ?

Behold me! From the time I bubbled up under the
seething wrath of the red volcano, a sea of fire, until
but a few fleeting years since — I, the King of the
stately peaks around me — I reigned unnoticed and
unknown! If the solitary hunter saw my rocky
top from afar in the sunset, or kindling to the moon,
he took me for some rosy cloud or glittering star
shining above a distant ocean of forest. Or if, per-
chance, he tracked the savage moose or black-cat
to my lonely glens, awed by my solitude and frightened by my wildness, he scarce dared to scan me,
or fasten my lonely throne in his remembrance.
And so the years went by. Did I sink in despair?
Did I forsake hope? No! I listened serenely
to the scream of the panther, and heard, undisturbed, the howlings of the tempest. If I launched
the eagle on my blast, it was not to lure human crea-
tures to my haunt, but to gaze myself on my own
majestic emblem. If I sent the wild wolf from
my gorges to howl around the cabin of the settler,
he was no messenger for him to visit my solitude.
Firmly did I breast the Winter's fury, and in de-
rision did I clutch his white mantle as he flew from
the bright presence of Spring, and, tearing it into
shreds, strew my glens throughout the year with
the fragments. I reared my cold brow to the Summer's beating heats, and robbed her also of her
most delicate blossom as a memento of hope ; and I

took my lessons from the smiling Spring. I saw on my breast, May hanging its tassels to the naked birch, and kindling its fire of promise on the boughs of the maple. And thus did the Spring speak to me : ' Courage,' she said, in her silver song. ' Hope on, hope ever. One day wilt thou be disrobed of thy savage loneliness, and be known among men. One day will the artist stamp thy form on immortal canvas, — the poet sing thee in imperishable numbers. Known wilt thou be, and honored. Thy panther's scream will give place to the soft tones of beauty, and the shriek of the eagle to the tinkle of the herd-bell and song of the ploughman in thy valleys. Life is around, and will soon awake thee from thy solitude into light and smiles.' "

" And true, O mountain," my heart made answer, " true is the lesson thou hast taught me. Henceforth, content shall be my aim, and anticipation my joy. Away the fiend Despair, and come, O angel of Hope. The present shall ever wear the rainbow, to irradiate my soul and tinge my future."

I was aroused from my reverie by the clink of a hammer. Merrill was chiseling my name, with his own and Robert's, into the granite of the mountain. And thus do we all seek to foil forgetfulness. Here, on the top of this savage peak, we hoped to rescue our memories from inevitable fate. A few seasons of rain and frost, and though deep the characters be cut, moss and lichen will creep into them, and, at last, bury them as securely as the grave will bury our frames of a day.

Suddenly, two reports sounded. Merrill and Robert had fired off their rifles for the echo. The sounds were like two short taps, or rather asthmatic coughs. A minute followed of blank silence — then a faint tone struggled from a distant gorge. And such is fame. We shout our names aloud to arrest the attention of the world, and lo, but stifled tones are heard, succeeded by a feeble reverberation, and all is still and soon forgotten.

The sounds proved the enormous height of the mountain, which soars to the breathless height of five thousand four hundred feet above tide — one glorious mile in the air.

I lingered upon the prospect till the lowering sun told his near setting. What a privilege to see the dying day from the summit of Tahawus. Slowly and grandly sank the Day-god to his rest. Not one by one, but in an instant, the peaks below were bathed in one vast blush. Soft looked Mount Colden in the light, soft as a bride, that stern mountain, and McIntyre above it gleamed like a ruby cloud. And the summit of Skylight, — sweet as a dream of love it smiled. The Dial's rounded diadem glowed in downy gold, and the frowning form of Dix's Peak looked as if steeped in carmined swansdown.

Slowly, slowly, slowly off it faded, — the daylight from every crest, — as if the light were loth to go. McIntyre shone the last, — the stony crag was the torch to light the Day-god to his rest, and the whole jagged summit turned sharply purple like the edges of a gem, against the gold and rosy glow.

If the sunset was glorious, the darkening of the peak-picture was grand. It seemed as if some mighty bird threw the shadow of his wings down upon it, as he slowly flew over the scene. The farther tops mingled in gloom, then nearer, nearer, nearer, nearer the shadow crept, until Haystack glimmered and it was night. Right over Tahawus came out a white orb like a spangle of snow, as if to watch it during the long night, its "sentinel-star."

How romantic would prove the night, to lie here on the brow of the stately Titan, listening to the long, deep breathings of its slumber, as the breeze heaved the forest, and waiting for the coming of the dawn !

Romantic, but awfully cold ! and so we began our descent. To encamp not far from the summit, though, for I was determined to see the sunrise as well as the sunset. So we left our area of several yards in extent, slid down the rocky dome, and, plunging into the forest, halted at a little dingle.

Here the ready axe of Merrill soon built a camp-fire, and his knife sheared hemlock-fringes for our couch under the expected moonlight.

Then, after a heartily enjoyed supper, we retired to our slumbers, my head filled with the sublime and beautiful sights of the day.

About midnight I awoke. A stealthy step had broken upon my dreams. I sat up. Step, step, step. I threw a brand; the form of an animal — a red cameo — was cut upon the gloom, and with a snarl it vanished. I then looked above. There glowed the full-orbed moon beaming, as at Lake Colden, like a friend's face, and full of comfort and gladness. In the crowded city she is lovely, amid the sights and sounds of pleasure. Sweetly does she glow upon the swelling sea when the tropic breeze bears balm and scent of all sunniest things; and upon the soldier in his night-watch, telling him of his home; vividly does her brow, so remembered in the old time, bring old scenes again to fill the heart with memories and the eye with tears; but here in the solitary woods (I never tire in the repetition of the thought), crowded with stately trees, sleeping on one ocean of leaves, and amid mountains watching the lonely denizens of their dingles, — how far more pure, more lovely, more sweet, more full of all holy memories, of all deep joys and cherished feelings! And here I became so confoundedly sleepy that I saw two moons, and, while wondering at the phenomenon, I fell back once more on my couch of hemlock and " slept the sleep that knows no waking " till the morning dawned.

Up with the earliest tint, and away to the mountain-top anew.

Gauzes of mist glimmered between the peaks, but the sky was clear as a crystal, the east a burnished gray. Soon the orient-glow announced the coming of the sun. The air was chilly, but not unpleasant. One little cloud shone like a flame-tinged jewel. All at once the Dial's leaning tower blazed as if a hidden fire had burst out. The grim mane of the crouching lion of Dix's Peak turned to mellow gold. Skylight glittered. Then peak after peak gleamed. The gauzes of the mist changed to gemmy tints. O, those exultant peaks ! how they broke into glory ! and then rose the sun ! What wonder that the antique mind deified the orb ! So grand, so glorious ! Helios harnessed his flashing steeds, in the poetic fancy of the Greek, for his daily pathway, and golden-haired Apollo sprang for his accustomed flight in the imagination of the Roman. And we of a purer faith, and nobler worship see in the dazzling splendor of the Day-god the shadow of " the Excellent Glory."

And now the yellow light hath bathed the brow of old Tahawus in one cheery smile! Hail, source of light and joy! Hail, Ithuriel of the golden spear that turns the swart demon of Night into the shining angel of Day! Man views thee with joy in the smoky city, but here, on the clear mountain-top, his heart leaps up to thee in pure delight and speechless admiration. Selah!

We returned to our dingle, and soon Merrill and Robert were busy in the ruby of the camp-fire preparing the morning meal. That secured, we started for the gorge between Tahawus and Haystack. Only one explorer [1] had visited it, and he but a few weeks before, and it possessed all the charm of newness.

The pleasant chirp of the mountain-finch, mingled with the bugle of the jay, accompanied our steps through the streak of forest next the rocky summit. In a few moments, we broke from its tangled covert, and stood upon the terrific slide of the mountain with other slides parallel. I looked back. The side of the Sky-Piercer had been scooped into a tremendous amphitheatre. From its brow, plunged manifold headlong torrents of stone, separated by strips of forest. Prominent above this awful hollow soared a headland. And here I must retrace my narrative.

[1] Henry B. Smith, D. D., Professor in the Union Theological Seminary, city of New York.

While listening to the pleasant silvery clink of Merrill's hammer carving our names on the peak, I saw a point or headland jutting out below where I stood. My fancy was fired at the sight. What awful gorge, what sublime expanse of landscape stretching dizzily away, would that rocky jut reveal? As there was no one that could answer that question but the jut itself, I resolved to reach it. An easy slope leading to a grassy carpet tempted my steps, and accordingly, I began to descend.

" Don't go there, I entreat ! " exclaimed Merrill. " It's dangerous."

The exclamation, instead of daunting, only whetted sharper my purpose. Besides, what danger lay in that easy slope and that grassy carpet. Consequently, disdaining the " small deer " advice of my guide, I persevered. The slope of rock was easy enough for a short distance, but what was my horror when I found that the grassy carpet turned out thick-branched, needle-bristling balsam bushes, just strong enough to sink me into their pointed torments, and scarcely strong enough to bear the tread.

Down I plunged into cavities of the sharp, stiff foliage, expecting, every moment, to encounter the green orbs of some panther; but, happily, I saw none. However, I persevered toward the jutting headland until I came to the most terrible twine of bayonet-pointed chevaux de frise I ever met in

all the woods. Down I sank in the tangled verdure, up I tilted, but little headway did I make.
There stood the headland, and here was I. At last
I became utterly discouraged, immersed as I was
in these prickly, agonizing branches, woven over
pits of jagged stones; so I turned back.   The
descent was comparatively easy, but the ascent, —
" ah, there's the rub!" Up I struggled, up through
the caverns of shaggy verdure where the wild cat
made his lair (or ought to have) ; up through the
sharp gullies of rock where I abandoned, for the
moment, my ladder of foliage ; then, forsaking the
gullies, up over or rather half wading through the
stiff layers of balsam, with the outline of a ravine on
my right. At last I reached the first slope of rock,
and the light chirp of Merrill's hammer again met
my ear, like the carol of the bluebird on the first
spring day.   It warmed my heart, that sharp,
sweet clink — and heartily glad was I to plant my
foot once more on the friendly peak. But to return.

What terrific convulsion had hollowed thus the
mountain-side to the quick ! I knew not; and after
a shudder at the appalling sight, I began the descent.

But before I did so, I turned for a farewell look
at the stately peak. As I gazed, an enormous
black eagle burst into sight, apparently from a small
cloud above. Down he swooped to the rocky pin-

nacle, where he stood, waving grandly his pinions as if responding to my adieu. He seemed the visible Spirit of Tahawus, receiving my homage. I could almost see the gold-tawny flash of his imperial eye. I did hear the trumpet of his majestic voice. " Farewell," he seemed to say, " child of an hour, and remember my precepts. Let not thy heart be cast down by trouble. Trust the future, and I command thee, whatever thy future, still cling to hope and have faith in Heaven. Farewell! long wilt thou remember me! In thy dreams will my lofty form be mirrored ; now, as thou seest me, and now black with the storm and wreathed with the blazing lightnings. Remember, that I bear a brave heart in my rocky bosom, and I scorn all that adverse fate can hurl against me! Farewell and remember ! "

He unfurled his bannery wings, he pointed his kingly beak, upward he soared, and, ere his voice ceased to echo in my soul, he vanished. Up as he flew, up I swept my arm, and my heart that seemed to soar with his majestic flight made answer : —

" Truly will I remember, O Spirit of Tahawus ; faith shall be my comforter and hope my guide ! Though fate may hurl its angriest blasts against me, and wrong and bitter injustice bar my pathway, still, remembering thee, will I bear upward my heart and steel my courage."

Again I turned for my descent. But finding the slide so steep and slippery, I took to the earth, where I found a recent trail. Down I went, preceded by my guides, down, until my ankles ached. Down, down still amid the twined forest, catching glimpses at either hand of the dark, rocky slides, until a gentle music told the Marcy Brook, one of the runlets stealing, mouse-like, from the foot of Tahawus.

Here lurked the Panther Gorge, northerly from where the trail crossed the little glassy brook. So we turned to track the rill to its source in the gorge. There was no more sign of this spot where we turned than at the Upper Works, and that fact explained why it was unknown. The trail wound from the brook directly away over Bartlett Mountain, the toe of Haystack, and one would as soon have turned aside, unless conscious of its existence, at any point between Lake Colden and Tahawus as at this.

After a tramp of a half mile through the pathless but by no means tangled woods, we saw, at our right, that Haystack was rearing itself as if for onslaught. On the left, old Tahawus seemed awed, for it showed no particular sign ; but at length, I saw a raw, gray, cracked precipice uplifting itself as if the mountain was aroused and was looking defiance. I then glanced at Haystack.

7

Up, up it towered as if to lift itself above the foe, and up, up soared Tahawus. Grim and threatening stood the two mountains, scowling at each other, as if summoning their energies for the dreadful strife. The loftier Tahawus soared, the loftier towered Haystack. Awful stillness reigned. My heart almost ceased its beatings. It seemed as if a stone, rattling from either mountain, would be the signal to hurl one against the other. The brook hid itself, as if in fear, under a rock. And now the two dread crags drew closer and closer. Loftier and loftier they soared, and closer and closer they drew together. In the black, frowning cleft, for it was now merely that, enormous crags, green with moss and crowned with trees, were piled in every shape, as if the two mountains had in old days clutched vast fragments from their breasts and dashed them against each other. Gloomier scowled the ravine and narrower it grew, while the rocks completely filled it. Yet above and through them I could see that the tortured mountains had at last locked themselves in a Titan struggle, falling upon their sides to do so. The gorge was at an end, a majestic *cul de sac*. We climbed the loftiest rock, and sought to look over the awful link, but in vain. Merrill then, with his clinking hammer, inscribed our names on the flinty tablet; we descended, and full to repletion with the terrific majesty of the gorge, soon repassed the two tangled miles and sat down to rest by the melodious brook. Sweetly sounded its fairy music, which soon restored the equilibrium of my spirits. I looked toward the terrible gorge. It seemed as if a mighty horror brooded over it; as if some demon made within it his black and scowling lair.

I hazard nothing in saying that this unknown, unthought-of gorge almost equals in sublimity the Indian Pass. The dizzy crags on either side soar nearly as lofty; the same terrible sense of awe and majesty reigns within it. As for the rocks, they seemed the very home of panthers, and I immediately named the chasm THE PANTHER GORGE.

> He steals with his gliding foot of air
> To the deer close-crouched in his brambly lair;
>
> A moment he fastens his famished gloat,
> Then leaps like a bolt to his victim's throat;
>> Savage Cat o' the mountain!
>
> Or he stretches his lithe frame, tawny and grim,
> For hours along the knotted limb;
>
> Then down he darts on his victim's back,
> And tears till it falls in its headlong track;
>> Savage Cat o' the mountain!
>
> He seeks his rough and rocky den,
> By day in the depths of the darksome glen;

But when the night puts on her crown,
He paceth up and he glideth down;
    Savage Cat o' the mountain!

His sorrowing whine, and his yell of fear
Startle the hunter's slumbering ear;

But again into slumber the hunter falls, —
His camp-fire daunting those blazing balls;
    Savage Cat o' the mountain.

O never the wolf, or moose, or bear,
The grapple fierce of their foe will dare!

But the trap that lurks in the matted shade
Maketh the monster sore afraid!
    Savage Cat o' the mountain!

For swift and sure is the hunter's aim,
And bringeth an end to that fiendish frame;

His brindled carcass then hangs on high,
Food for the hovering wings of the sky;
    Savage Cat o' the mountain!

We left the little glossy brook to find its way to the Ausable; now burrowing like an otter within choking branches, now gliding like a water-rat through grassy banks, and now lurking, like a mink, among floating logs, till it joins the river.

Up, up Bartlett Mountain we went, until my knees shook, and my feet pained me. Half way above, I turned for a farewell gaze at Tahawus. Stately and awful was the form of the old scarred Warrior-king on the sky, a scowling Thunder-cloud. What a grand mountain! Lifting its wrinkled brow of hypersthene into the region of the snow-flake it fills the region, for miles, with its frown. Full is it of sublime gorges, sweeping amphitheatres, soaring crags, torrent-like slides, and horrible abysses. And yet it owns pines that sing like the sea, brooks that warble like the robin, and flowers that scent the air, like the orange-blossoms of Italy. It even condescends to own the little Marcy Brook.

And " Farewell, farewell! " I murmured. " Thy mighty voice I hear no longer, but thy wise lessons are graven on my heart. Farewell, farewell, but not, I trust, forever. Again will I seek thy majestic peak, O monarch of the storm! and again list thy thunderous music! And when home delights shall twine me, then, in dreams of the night, shall I behold thee glaring in the lightning and smiling in the sun! Farewell, O farewell, grand conqueror of a thousand storms! majestic master of a glorious realm! Soft art thou in thy love, but O how terrible in thy wrath! Farewell, but not forever! "

At last we reached the summit of the mountain, still following the faithful trail to which our feet had clung since we left the Upper Works, and then descended. How my knees did quiver and my ankles ache! Down, down we went, until I thought the whole world had fallen sidewise and

I was doomed to go down it. A hundred times I thought I saw the sparkle of the Upper Ausable Pond through the close trees. But no! the pitiless Merrill and ditto Bob still descended. In fact, I rather thought Bob enjoyed the joke. O the "long, long, weary" trail to that Pond. Suddenly Merrill stopped.

" I thought I saw the glitter of the Upper Ausable !" said he ; " but I guess it was only a white birch or two shining in the sun."

And so it is in the woods. Often, in the green gloom, a glitter will smite your eye like water, but a nearer inspection resolves it into a white birch or wild poplar, shaking its leaves like the play of water in some transient sigh of the forest — for forests sigh as do men and women in this world of ours. But at length a little wren of a brook began singing. I thought it was a multitude of mountain-finches at first, but the chirp was too continuous, and at last it blended into a delicious murmur — a hum like the tone of the pine.

" The Shanty Brook," said Merrill. Another rill from Haystack, touching its little lute, to bury itself, like its brother, the Marcy, in the River Ausable.

The Shanty Brook! and it put me in mind of the shanty, most welcome of nests! At last the trail suddenly turned, or rather another trail intersected it from the east in a sharp angle. A fractured stump, like a post, stood at the intersection, — most picturesque of sign-boards, — and on a rough shingle were two lines, at first difficult as a Delphic oracle.

" Tou reite Mountt Mairc, lefft Upr Ousobl Pond. Reite onn Sothe Lour Ousobl, aynd thin ovr Pond tou Keyne Flatt."

(Pond was the only word spelled right by chance, or rather because it could not, by any chance, be spelled wrong.)

" Merrill, read this, will you ? I'm so tired I cannot ! "

" To right Mount Marcy. Left Upper Ausable Pond. Right on south, the Lower Ausable ; and then over Pond to Keene Flats ! "

" Just so ! " replied I. " We will go to the Upper Ausable ; " and we went. It was a short distance only to the Pond, and Merrill began another bubble of a shanty for our night's encampment while Robert busied himself in cutting shanty-wood.

All the quiet, yellow afternoon I sat at the border of the beautiful lake, embosomed as it was in mountains four thousand feet high. A plunge in the crystal — a water-rat diving. Another — a gem of a duck. Another " squtter "(Bob's word) — a whole fleet of ducks, as black as otters and swift as loons. They made the voyage of a point. Then a breeze dipped its plumes, and then with a meek ripple, a crane, looking meeker, waded from the shore and gobbled up a fish. Meek men gobble up their own species sometimes, and therein they are worse than cranes. How men do prey on one another. Not only as regards money, but reputation. How often does the stealthy slander, whence no one knows, destroy character if not life. Like the good Baldur, in the Scandinavian Edda, who was slain by the mistletoe the blind Hodur threw, how many a reputation has been destroyed by a slander springing from shadow.

Here and there, on the very brink of the pond, stood the mountain-ash or moose-missee, grasping the crag and picturing on the water the red blaze of its berries, kindling the nook where it stood like a bonfire, and seeming to throw a splendor even over the incipient tints of the September woods.

We despatched Robert, as soon as the shanty was completed, to the nearest settlement (Phineas Beedy's) at the head of the Keene Flats, for provisions, our stock being exhausted. His return we expected in about four hours. The time passed but he came not. While watching the poetic effects of the bright pond, I was conscious of crannies in my stomach that yielded very unpoetic twinges. As for Merrill, he writhed like a black-snake, and looked like the genius of colic.

At last, about sundown, as we sat where a smudge was sending its light breath to puff away the black-flies, Merrill exclaimed plaintively (people are very plaintive when hungry), —

" What on earth has become of the boy ? " As I couldn't answer, and echo wouldn't, his inquiry was lost.

" He hasn't met with a panther, has he ? " continued Merrill, this time very plaintively, and biting a blade of blue-joint in default of an onion.

Not being gifted with seeing things not to be seen, I again answered not.

" Bless my soul ! " said Merrill, very pathetically, " I'm so hungry I could eat tadpoles ! "

I told him his dinner was handy by, but as he didn't show any alacrity in securing it, I concluded he never ate tadpoles.

At last, at sundown, we started on the trail to the lower Ausable Pond in search of the lost boy. The level light lay pleasantly on the bushes and dingles of our way, tinging the wild sunflowers and silver-weeds either side the trail, but my weakness, consequent upon hunger, was so distressing that the mile seemed longer than the ascent of Tahawus. We crossed a brook on a fallen sycamore, and at length emerged upon the pond. We entered on an area of ghastly sand, veined by a black, sluggish stream, and thinly scattered with white, ghostly trees. The brook (the commencement of the River Ausable's[1] East Branch) linked the two ponds. We had seen it at our right, throughout our trail, dashing and brawling along.

Humiliating as the admission is, I did not even glance at the scenery, in the pangs of my hunger, and therefore listened to the whoop of Merrill with an anxiety only relieved by an answering whoop, ringing, clear as a bell, from the pond.

"Robert!" ejaculated Merrill, "just below old Indian Face! Hurrah!"

Hurrah it was, although what old Indian Face could be, I neither knew nor cared.

In a few minutes, the boy appeared in a boat winding through the Stygian stream, and seating ourselves on a dark log, we watched, after he had landed, the unfolding of his knapsack's contents. First a half dozen of smooth, rosy-skinned onions; then a wedge of tawny pork, and then a few loaves of brown, crusty bread.

If ever I ate food with a relish, I did after I had peeled my white, beautiful onion. The rich pungency was truly delightful. As for Merrill, his eyes bulged at every twist of his mouth as though he saw spectres.

We discussed our viands, and felt the strength

[1] A French word signifying River of Sand, said to be derived from a sandy bar at the river's mouth.

again in our limbs and the courage in our hearts.
I wonder if Alexander would have fought on an
empty stomach ! While pondering this interesting
question, I vow and declare if I didn't forget the
scenery once more, and only thought of it when
safe back at the shanty.

Our vegetables proving but appetizers, we instantly began providing for our supper. Slicing our
white and rosy pork, we toasted it on sweet lim-
ber sprays of birch ; we fried our onions until they
floated in golden curls, and distilling our black tea
(the only beverage, I repeat, desirable in the
woods), we were soon pleasantly engaged.

The sun had now sunk. I went to the pond
again to enjoy the scenery. And what scenery !
The Upper Ausable is a cup of water in a big bowl
— that is, with its mountains. And such mountains ! Sheer from the level of the pond they soar
four thousand feet, if not five, throwing their sable
shade, at this hour, entirely over the sheet, and
literally excluding the sun at five in the afternoon
in summer, and about four in autumn (in winter I doubt whether it shines there at all) ; and
letting its morning light be seen at eight in summer, and nine in autumn. Over these mountains
lies the shortest route to the stately gorge (nearly
equal, I hear, to the Indian Pass) of the Dial, which
I hoped to tread before my jaunt was over, but as

the route was simply horrible, I concluded to try the longest way, by Root's. And here I fell into one of my fits of dreaming again. I personified that gorge. I pictured a grim monster towering to the clouds; in one hand a thunder-cloud, and in the other a slide, frowning downward upon the intruder, and asking, in a terrific blast, "Why can't people keep out of my way! plague take 'em!" and here my dream was cut short by my feeling something very wet where I was seated, and I found it was my confounded coat-tail dipping intô the water. I whirled it up and startled off a duck at the same time; and what a duck! What gems of feathers; what yellow feet; what a white under-shape; what silken tints of neck, and what a plumy crown!

The clear twilight thickened, the round moon rose. "I say, Robert, have the scow ready!" (There was an old swine of a scow wallowing in the mud of the margin.) "I'll take a moonlight sail in these bright waters!"

We raised the old swine, with many a hollow suck and gasp from its wallow, and steered into the pond. But if you wish to enjoy the romantic, never sail on a moon-kindled water in a scow. Up sprang the mountains, and the ripples sang, and the seraph above beamed and blessed my senses; but, after all, don't try the scow. What profound peace, what heavenly quiet! "Why Merrill, what is the matter. We were floating in the moonlight a moment ago, and here we are in water black as a Fisher.

So we returned the scow to its "wallowing in the mire," entered the shanty, and slept.

CHAPTER V.

WHITEFACE.

Lower Ausable Pond. — Old Indian Face. — The Slide. — Road to
the Keene Valley. — Moonlight on Whiteface. — Whiteface Clove.
— Return to Scott's.

THE morning ushered in stern work. The
Keene Flats were to be reached and partly traversed
before night. So we started. The mile of carry
between the two ponds was passed, and we then embarked on the Ausable River Branch (the Lower
Ausable Pond being a half mile in front), in Robert's boat of the day before. After twisting the
distance, with dead scenes around, but gorgeous
views in front, we opened upon the pond. To
think that an onion could divert my attention, as it
did yesterday, from one of the most sublime exhi-
bitions of scenery in the State !

The Lower Ausable Pond lurks, like a dark drop,
in the bottom of a mountain chalice, and the sun
gilds the world without, an hour before it climbs even
to the rim of this chalice. Or, have you seen the star
at the foot of the blue aster's goblet ? So shines
the Lower Ausable in the depth of its mountain-

cup. Black gleams the water, and the ripple from the oar glitters like a diamond.

" Old Indian Face ! " said Robert, giving a deeper dip than usual to his oar, whereby the dugout cleaves the wave as the trout cleaves the stream.

Aha, thought I, I'll see it.

" Where is it, Robert ? "

Rob pointed to a ragged cliff of red stone where manifold fissures were indented.

" I don't see any face, or even a hint of one," said I.

At this moment the boat turned. Sure enough, there was a vast profile in the red, mellow rock; and not only that, but below, another outline showing like a pappoose ; the whole gigantic cameo kindled golden in the sun.

How sublime, I thought, that nature should thus have carved the eternal rock into a likeness which remains as an imperishable memento of a powerful race driven almost from the earth by one more powerful.

The following is the legend of the Rock : —

Ages ago the wild and warlike Ta-ha-wi ruled the region, subjecting the Saranacs around their beautiful lakes, shaped like the forehead of the antlered deer, and even carrying their sway to the distant Eagle Wings at Wandah, or Lake of Light.[1]

[1] Little Tupper's Lake.

Their Sachem dwelt at the Lower Ausable Pond, called by them the Dark Cup, while the village of the tribe stood at the Lake of the White Water Lily, their name for the Upper Ausable.

But though wild and fierce were the tribe, the Sachem was kind and gentle. His virtues shone around him as the stars shine about the moon. He had been a great warrior in his youth, bold as the roused eagle; in his old age, the eagle had changed to the beaver.

His one daughter, the wife of a young brave who fell in a fight with the Saranacs, had died, leaving him a grandchild, who bid fair to take the place of his father in the war-trail. But he also sickened and died. Then the old chief's heart broke. He assembled his people one sunset round his lodge, at the foot of the red rock now bearing his likeness, and thus he spoke:

" Adota [1] is old. He is broken. Long has it been since he could send the arrow. Once it flew from him to the heart of the foe, like the glance of the sunshine, and sounding like the hiss of the yellow pine in the wind. Then he was young, the brave of a hundred war-paths. Did he shrink from the Saranacs? Was his war-song silent in the lodges of the Eagle Wings? No! His tomahawk flashed from the Lake of the Clustered Stars,[2] and over the

[1] The Bow.   [2] Lower Saranac Lake.

waters of the Silver Sky [1] to the Lake of Wandah. But Adota grew as you now see him, my people. Ja-ko-wa,[2] the bride of his youth, went at the call of Ha-wen-ne-yo, but she left Wo-ne-da.[3] The lodges of my people rang with drum and flute, the words of warriors and the songs of maidens, when Wo-ne-da entered, as a bride, the wigwam of Ka-je-wa.[4] But where are now Wo-ne-da and Ka-je-wa? Did ye see the flowers of the moose-wood in the days of blossoms, around the Lake of the Lily? Where are they? and where the bride and her chieftain?" and the Sachem's voice wailed like the wind in the moon of Rainbows.[5] "Yet O-jis-ta [6] was left to sparkle on the darkness that rested in the lodge of Adota. O my people!" and here his tones were keen as the wind in the season of snows over the crag above him, "the small sparkle no longer sheds joy on the heart of Adota. Ha-wen-ne-yo loved him too much to let the little star glitter on earth; he put the sparkle on his own forehead. Like yon red spear (pointing to a darting streak which at that moment cleft a cloud scowling in the west like Mount Sinai of old flashing with its lightnings and muttering with its thunders), O-jis-ta shone and vanished. Farewell, my people! Adota longs for the immortal strawberry! He has asked

---

[1] Upper Saranac Lake.   [2] The Dove.   [3] The Moon.
[4] Warclub.   [5] October.   [6] The Star.

8

Ha-wen-ne-yo to take him, and he goes.   Farewell, farewell ! "

As he spoke, he waved his arm, he raised his eyes, and fell backward.   To him sprang his oldest chieftains, but in the gray twilight they saw their Sachem was dead.

Higher rose the cloud ; thicker gleamed the lightning ; more dread the voice of the thunder ; keener and wilder the blast.

And, as the people still stood in sorrow around their Sachem, a grand glare of lightning opened, and a long, deep, solemn roll of thunder sounded. Round the Dark Cup it echoed and echoed, until in repeated tones it died toward Tahawus, Piercer of the Heavens.   So wild the glare, so dread the sound, the people shuddered.   Then spake Kaiwa,[1] the Great Medicine of the tribe, falling on his knee, and lifting his long right arm to the darkened zenith :

" Tribe of the Ta-ha-wi ! " said he, and his tones were full of the profoundest reverence, — " in yon lightning shone to me the terrible eye of Ha-wen-ne-yo, and my ears still ring with the awful volume of his voice.   ' My children,' said the voice, ' I have taken Adota to the Happy Hunting Grounds, where he is now tasting the strawberry from the hands of Ja-ko-wa and Wo-ne-da, with the beams of O-jis-ta shining on his heart.   But though the Sachem has

[1] The Sky.

left his people, I will give a token to my children, the Ta-ha-wi, by which they shall remember Adota to the latest generations.' "

The priest ceased. Then burst the storm with lightning and thunder, blast and rain. A strange shudder shook the earth. The Dark Cup foamed and roared in the darkness.

The tribe cowered in the woods, and when the storm vanished their return was swift to the village by the Lake of the Lily.

As Kah-qua[1] fired the heavens with his blazing eye-ball, an Indian direct from the Dark Cup entered the village with a tale of wonder. They listened, and with rapid feet traversed the trail between the two waters. Soon the red rock opened upon their view, and lo! on its summit stood Kai-wa pointing to the face of the crag turned toward the Cup. And there, songs to Ha-wen-ne-yo! there appeared the features of Adota, and there also were those of O-jis-ta resting upon the heart of the Sachem.

The tribe buried the old chief beneath his rocky profile, his immortal monument, and there they held their most solemn festivals, until, wasted by their wars, scourged by disease, and encroached upon by civilization in its rough shape of hunter and trapper, they vanished from the region.

[1] The Sun.

Passing Old Indian Face we almost immediately came to the foot of the wild, dark pond where the river flowed out. On our left stood a deserted log-hut.

" That's old Hale's," said Robert, " but the old man 's not there now. He went two mile further in, just before the valley begins."

" What made him move ? " asked I.

" A slide," returned Robert.

" Well, how was it ? "

" There had been four or five days of rain, and one night, 'twas as black as my hound Pitt's mouth, and old Hale was just about going to bed. All of a sudden, he heard a noise, — a rattling, crashing, thundering kind of noise, — so he jumped, I tell ye, as spry, for an old man, as a squirrel ; and Jehosa-phat ! what did he see but the whole mountain back of him a coming down hill like a trotting moose. Trees, rocks, earth, and water, and everything else, tumble-te-tumble ! Fire flashed just like tinder, and the old fellow gave up, supposing his family and all the rest of creation would be burst up, when the slide split into two forks, leaving him on an island. Down plunged the slide into the pond, with a clatter-de-spatter that brought out old Indian Face bright as 'twere on the black, like a flash o' lightnin', and then 'twas all over. The old fellow, however, was so awfully scared, that he skedaddled

from the pond, and built a shanty two miles this side
of Phin Beedy's. We'll pass it on our way to
Keene Flats."

We left the dug-out, with the oars perking up
its sides like a terrier's ears. Here we dropped
our delicate thread of trail that, like the clew of
Ariadne, had guided us through the labyrinth of
forest, from our starting-point at Scott's.

We mounted a steep hill, and a pleasant wood-
road, inviting our feet downward, lay before us,
leading to the paradise of the Keene Valley. The
thick forest twined still on either side, but there
was a track telling of wood-carts ; we knew the
forest would soon give place to meadow and grain-
field, and we strode lightly onward. Soon we came
to Gill Brook, one of the streams of the valley entering the Ausable River. On its bank sat an
artist, transferring the picturesque beauties of the
scene to his canvas. He was not aware of our
presence until we were over him.

"How are you?" said Merrill.

Now this guide of mine, although a good-looking
fellow in the main, was, at this particular juncture,
about as faithful an image of a slouching Italian
bandit as I would wish to see. I looked like an
outlaw, and Robert was a scarecrow — all good
enough company for wild-cats, but hardly pre-
sentable to civilized beings.

The artist lowered his brush and lifted his head.

" Ah — ah — pret — ah — hum ! " said he. Entering into the natural feelings of the startled artist, I blandly said, —

" A lovely scene you are copying ! "

" Ah — ah — pretty well, I thank you. How are you ? "

We left him, after an examination of his beautiful painting, full of golden lights and purple shadows, and skimmed onward.

A mile more brought us to a picnic, — the gay colors of the ladies' dresses contrasting with the umber of the road-track, and green of the foliage.

After leaving the party, openings began to occur in the woods — symptoms of the Valley. A field broke out, then an expanse of meadow, then a small farm with the homestead in the grassy lane. At last, we mastered a knoll, and a rough clearing, with a log-cabin, met our view.

" Old Hale's," said Robert.

The old fellow stood by a stack of India-wheat, with a patched felt hat giving him a frightened look, as if he anticipated another slide.

A jeweled rooster, a superb duck, and a brown partlet or two were strutting and scratching around ; a pig " humphed " in a log-pen, and a goose nibbled the short grass of the knoll, all yielding a tame, domestic look to the circling woods. An open gate shortly afterward ushered us to the brow of a cleared amphitheatre, with a dwelling at the right of the steeply descending track.

" Phineas Beedy's ! " said Merrill.

It was a beautiful rural picture indeed. Hill-sides, richly red with the stacked India-wheat, sloped at either hand, forming a vast dingle with the house in the midst, while the tall, wooded summits of the Keene Range looked like sentinels upon the scene. The whole was glowing in the light of the after-noon — that magic hour when the slanting sunshine is more yellow, and the streaming shadows more richly black, than at any other period of the day.

We halted at Beedy's a half hour, and then re-sumed our way. Here was the head of the en-chanting Keene Valley. Stretching thirty or forty miles to Lake Champlain, it embosoms, as the Au-sable Valley, the East and West Branches of the wild, fierce Ausable, that never forgets its birth-spots in the Indian Pass, the mountain-meadow of Tahawus, and the crag-crowned Upper and Lower Ausable, — a stately birth indeed ! The Branches unite at the village of The Forks, and the river veins the valley to where it whitens and blackens through the " Walled Rocks," near Keeseville, and then wends its meadowy way to the Lake.

We had now left the forest, and henceforth our

jaunt was to be through the wide India-wheat fields, kine-grazed pastures, and pleasant home-steads of the rural valley, until just before we should reach old Whiteface, our next point.

Did I regret the exchange! Indeed did I! The valley features could be seen anywhere in our noble State, but the wild forest was nowhere but just where it was. Notwithstanding a vivid recollection of its fatigues and hardships, including the semi-starvation at the Upper Ausable, I clung with a loving heart to the memories of its grandeur, its beauty, its silence, its loneliness, its diamond waters, its dells, dingles, glades, and vistas, its colonnaded trees, its one trail, its eagles' nests, its hawks' nests, its ravens, its jays, its finches, its arbors, its crags, and, above all, its wild, joyous freedom — freedom from all restraint, from all the conventionalities, cares, sorrows, and mockeries of the world.

Leaving the Beedy dingle we entered upon a beautiful, open glade, with the pebbly East Ausable gliding at our left or west, between banks fringed and grouped pleasantly with splendid sycamores and maples. Beedy's stream, another ooze or runlet from the mountains, came in at our right, to mingle also with the Ausable. And now I realized how deftly the elastic forest soil helps along the tread; for the road here was sunk in sand, and I can safely say my two miles' tramp jaded me more than thrice the distance in my forest threading. A glow, however, seemed to permeate Nature, — the beautiful charm which Cultivation yields, notwithstanding the superior attraction (to me) of the wilderness.

" The Noon Mark comes out plain this evening," said Merrill, pointing to a crest, three thousand feet high, upon our right, among a cluster of peaks, " and there is Rogers' Mountain ; " looking at another elevation. Tall mountains both, but, in comparison with the giants that had filled my heart and taken away my breath, poplars to pine-trees.

A gray shower was unfurling its misty pinions in a distant stretch of field at the west, but the brown sand clutched my feet so closely, I in vain essayed a swifter gait.

A slender rain soon glittered on the farther prospect, but it wafted itself to the range of hills at the north, where it filmed the sharp outlines, without troubling itself with us. Hill-born, it clung to the hills. Its moist breath was however manifest in the deeper perfume of the air, and in the softening of the sun-glow, so that my onward path was comparatively pleasant.

Sundown was gilding the west as we passed several charming dwellings nested in trees, with grass-carpets extending to the road-side. The frequent well, with its long angular sweep, told of a cold water region; and the apple-trees were turning to rosy and tawny tints in the most appetizing manner. At last we stayed our steps at a pleasant homestead on the road's left. We were at Holt's, our resting-place for the night.

Twilight's tinge, " the blind man's holiday," shone on the sylvan valley. To the southeast, Dix's Peak and the Dial wrestled with the haze that rested transparently on the near prospect, while the neighboring Noon Mark asserted itself more boldly. In front and rear smiled the smooth green fields, dotted with trees, where the flock bleated, the herd tinkled, and the horse stamped and whinnied. Brown Rurality sat under his homestead-trees, with the sickle in his tired grasp, enjoying, after his harvesting, the golden leisure of the sinking day. And now a star opens. Night steals from the deepening east with an eye to the vanishing light, waiting to put on her tiara of stars. And soon, under the shelter of her blessed reign, I retired to rest.

No one, but those experiencing, can realize the pleasurable sensations of peeling off clothes, worn day and night for a fortnight, and the soft feel of a civilized bed in a civilized room. My blue, thick hunting-shirt had clung so closely to my frame for the above period, that, when I stripped myself, it seemed taking the skin (pain excepted) with it. But, with all this, there was a vast deal wanting; the fragrant and elastic spruce and hemlock fringes of my wild-wood couch, and the free, fresh, flowing atmosphere, redolent of all forest scents; the star-glow of night, the rose-flush of dawn, the melodies of trees, the soft murmurs of winds; and with these reflections I glided into sleep.

The next morning brought with it the consciousness that I was in the valley, not the forest.

The frequent bleat, the occasional bellow, the glad voices of children, and the passing whistle, filled the air.

My destination was now Whiteface, with horse-muscles instead of man's, through the smooth valley. In the sheen of the morning, after a plentiful breakfast, my guides and I stood at Holt's porch, awaiting the wagon, our conveyance to the mountain.

" Do you see the Dial out there ? " asked Holt.

There it stood, with its rocky head wearing a hat of mist slouched almost to its rounded shoulders.

" We call it the Noon Mark here, sometimes," continued he. " But we have another Noon Mark," pointing to the mountain I have before noticed, " and we call it so, from the sun standing directly over it at twelve o'clock."

I bade a regretful adieu to several most delightful people, both male and female, acquaintance with
whom one evening had ripened, on my part, and
I trust on theirs, into warm friendship, and off
my wagon started through the beautiful valley,
shining with cultivation and glossed in the matin
sun.   No fences were visible, for cattle are re-
strained from roaming the fields of neighbors;
consequently my eye travelled unrestricted over
broad tracts of the stacked India-wheat and golden
rye.

"Teams" passed us, the drivers holding red
reins, which, from their frequency, amounted to a
feature of the valley.   Our wheels wafted us over
the level track like a boat in water.   An odd-
shaped mound, a grassy rampart (formed doubtless
by the action of water), in a broad meadow, as if
used to resist a foe's attack, greeted us at our left.
The sun steeped it pleasantly, and I could not but
remark the contrast between its probable tumult,
" long time ago," and the present blandness and
quiet.   Another the valley owns, identical with its
brother, at the angle where the road winds up the
hill at the left toward the ascent of the Keene
Mountains on the way westward to Scott's.

On the smooth wheels wheeled until this last
rampart appeared.   Here the road turned another
mile or two eastward, and the little village of Keene

dotted the landscape. After a half hour's sojourn, we again started. Swerving into another road, we now left the valley at an angle. We passed the dread signs of a water-spout which a terrific tempest poured out upon the valley of the East Ausable River.

" 'Twas an awful bad time," said the driver. " Two human creeters drowned for sarten."

His description, however, was cut short by a shower which drifted past us. I have earlier noticed the prevalence of these showers in this mountain region. They appear to lie in wait in the manifold gorges and hollows, to creep out and blot the landscape for a minute, and then scud back to their lairs.

We had, as before remarked, left the valley at the road-angle, and broken ground spread on either side the wheel-track, monotonous and unpicturesque.

We at length reached the pretty little village of Upper Jay, within which another prowling shower was pelting. As we turned into another road, after quitting the village, which brought us in full view of grand old Whiteface on our right, a third shower, nay, a perfect storm of rain, suddenly dashed upon us.

It seemed as if the stern mountain was warning us from his summit, — dashing his full goblet of cold water in our faces to daunt us back from his savage fastnesses. But seeing that we intended to persevere, he doubtless made a virtue of necessity, and threw a sheaf of golden arrows directly from his pinnacle over the gray, wet landscape. Out flashed the jeweled scene, and with it, rose our spirits. A wagon in our rear, which had glimmered ghostlike through the rainy haze, a tent of umbrellas, glowed now a little moving picture.

A few miles more brought us to the mountain's east base, where lived Hickock, who, with commendable energy, had cut a road nearly straight to the crest. In fact, it is so steep on account of its straightness, that the only wonder is he did not tumble over backward while performing his task.

At four o'clock in the afternoon (after a rustic and excellent dinner at Hickock's, in which the freshest and sweetest vegetables, all nicely cooked, predominated), under a sky of burnished blue, swept clean and naked by the shower, I started, with my guides, and Hickock as our pioneer, for the tip-top of the mountain.

We passed a rough field or two in the rear of Hickock's dwelling, and, crossing the Ausable River by a wooden bridge, entered a smooth, grassy glade of the forest at the foot of the Titan. Up the ascending track (here a broad one) we went in single file. The ascent was, as yet, not difficult ·

we were only on,the instep of the mountain. But
the tall pines and stone-cedars seemed to say, in
the fanning breeze, " A happy time you'll have in
tugging up old Whiteface, won't you ? um, um,
um, hiss ! " And the hopple-bushes and wood-
sprouts quivered in the ground-currents with laughter at the thought, while a splendid red mercury-
vine on a tall tree fairly shook its sides.

Soon there was a white flashing among the
leaves, with a pleasant rumble crumbling on the
ear ; a mountain-stream leaping down among its
green rocks, bearing tidings, in the foam of its descent, as to the steepness of its birthplace. No
name had yet been affixed to the torrent, but, as I
saw it glittering in its craggy home, I named it
" The White Ribbon." And now Old Surly Face
shows his real steepness.

Sundown sinks and twilight steals — scarce twilight, for the faithful moon tenders her silver torch.
The faithful, beautiful moon ! How sweetly and
tenderly had she clung to my nights from the beginning of my wanderings, glorifying the gloom of
the terrific forests ! Blessings upon her !

Now for a moonlight tug up the Giant's shoulders
eastward. Occasional glades unfold, letting in
gleams of the delicate lustre, while broader vistas
unloose the eye over an expanse of illumined
wood. Rough stems near by are sleeked over by

the smooth, white sheen, while the path, now diminished to a slender trail, is a bright streak, and the lichened rocks are glossy. A pure enamel coats the moss of the pine-tree's sandal. Now and then deep, dead shocks are heard, — the low thunder of the falling decayed trees. No turning, but straight upward with continuous strain. Straight as the honey-bee's flight, or the robin's. Evidently, Hickock fastened his eye to the top, and to the top he went (as well as he could), " straight as a string." A little more turning and less directness, Hickock! So up, hour after hour, we climb, resting occasionally against a rock or tree-stem. Surely we are at the top. Not yet.

" You think this here mite o' ground steep, don't ye ? " said Hickock, as I slipped, in clambering up an ascent blunt as a lynx's snout.

" Well, it's no more to be named at the same time o' day with a spot up thereaway, than a puff-ball with a pipping apple ! "

That spot haunted Hickock.

" It is rayther steep here, isn't it ? " said he.

" Ah — ah — ah — yes, confoundedly so ! " panted I.

" It's no more to be named at the same time o' day with that spot up there, than a chipmuck with a painter ! "

" Well, now, I der say you think this bit o'

ground steep, don't ye?" again said he, as I was tugging, on my hands and knees, up a knoll like a great muskrat's head, and slippery at that.

"'Cause it's no more to be named at the same time o' day with that Dutch ruff up there; than an artichoke with mush and molasses!" chuckling.

By and by I saw an ascent like a grenadier's cap.

"We don't go up that place, Hickock, surely!"

"That's jest the place we do go up! Why, that's the place I've been tellin' you of!"

I am certain Hickock took a fiendish delight in encountering that spot. I can fancy the chuckle with which he carried the trail on his hands and knees up the precipice, for it is little else! He might have made steps in it while he was about it. "Ha, ha, ha! tired are ye, folks?" I hear him, in imagination, soliloquize as he cuts the trail. "Well, I'll make ye tireder! Jest you climb up here, won't ye! You think, you city folks, to come out here into the woods and scare us, hay! to go up our mountings" (a good name by the way), "and a kinder dance up, one, two, three, four, and five. You jest try to climb up these mountainous regions, and specially up this mite o' ground, that's like a little dog's tail straight up. Aha, well, now git up or rayther, claw up, and be plagued to ye!"

I did claw up (I had serious thoughts of taking my teeth to it), and — by Jove, here's the top!

9

No! only a clearing with a shanty lurking in a deep hollow, like a dottle at the bottom of a pipe-bowl.

I rest in the shanty, while my guides cut shanty-wood. The silver mantle of the moon covered the clearing so pleasantly, and I was so wearied, that I determined to forego the pearly picture of the landscape kneeling in the moonlight, proffered from the summit of Whiteface, particularly as the ascent involved the descent; for it is one thing to see moon-lit views from the tops of mountains, and another to sleep there.

Shortly, preparations are made for the night. The camp-fire is built on the edge of the hollow, and kindled with matches.

What a burst of brilliancy over the clearing! Every tree and stump is visible, drawn in hair-lines on the wild crimson of the fire! What genial warmth, what consoling, heart-reaching comfort!

We take our wild-wood supper, and then occupy the shanty, I soon entering in Bryant's

> " Land of Dreams,
> With steeps that hang in the twilight sky."

Morning.

" Clear, Merrill ? "

" Cloudy.   Threatens rain."

" Bad.   But hurrah for a lunch, and then for a speedy ascent!"

We start, and press upward. A half mile is

passed through the rapidly diminishing trees, and we emerge upon the bare summit, — a long ridge running northeasterly, with a sudden dropping of the prospect — I feeling that thrilling of the nerves before experienced by me on the brow of Wall-face. We ascend the ridge, also a steep, widening, but low cone, with a spacious area at the top, and the pinnacle is won.

It is rocky, patched, and seamed with soil, and scattered with ledges forming apertures or caverns. In a hollow of the rocks, stone walls had been rudely built, with boards laid on top — a mountain shanty. Moss and grass, with harebells, golden-rods, and pearls of cinquefoil, as at Tahawus, meander along the crevices, and make mosaic of the mosses, while bitter blueberries are scattered about.

And is not the sight worth the labor of the climb? At first, all is one vast stretch of mist, an ocean over which are thickly scattered mountain-tops like islands. A magnificent prospect indeed, with the vapor lending it vagueness and mystery. Such might have been chaos, ere " the Spirit of God moved upon the waters." Through the lower mist float denser shapes of fog, like the first attempts at organic life that chaos might have produced.

All below, under a dull, cloudy sky, is gray, except the dark summits.

The scene is grand; but can forms of grace and

beauty be born from that confused mighty mass, that boundless, disordered sea?

A bleak chilliness, too, pervades the air, which is open, brisk, and bracing, like the elastic freshness of the just vanished thunder-storm.

But the mist rises — it curls upon the summits that seem like smoking altars.   Higher it ascends; it mingles with the sky.   And — lo! — from an opening in the east darts the morning light!

And see! a multitude of pinnacles with one peak soaring over all, rosy in the sunrise!   Aha! Tahawus, kinging it over his realm as usual!

What shines immediately below!   Lake Placid, by all that is beautiful!   And what a silver painting!

All about are crests burning in the light, like the Angels of the Alleluiah in the splendors of the Throne.

What is that outline rounding down like

> "the new moone
> Wi' the auld moone in hir arme!"

The portal of the Indian Pass!   Soft as love, and sweet as hope!   Well, I will never trust appearances again!   That, the gate of the Indian Pass, the savage, scowling demon of the wilds!   It looks as if it would melt at the gaze!   And that summit! It is McIntyre!   It seems a girl's vision!   Why not name it " The Maiden's Dream!"   I think I see the old mountain grin, wide as the Pass at his foot, at the thought!

But there is a real dream of beauty and softness, there where the amber light rests in lovelier lustre than on all the rest of the prospect. The Keene Valley, sweet as the roses of Damascus to the pilgrim of the desert, pillowing its head upon the feet of the Ausable Mountains, and bathing its broad green sandals in the lake of Corlear.[1]

What chain of flashing waters is yonder! The Saranac Lakes, the Racket River, Big Tupper's Lake, and Little Tupper's, — the wolf-haunted and panther-guarded.

But we cannot stay here much longer, for the brief sunlight has faded, and it is beginning to rain. So we turn our faces downward; and in a short time we reach the clearing.

"What a beautiful bird!"

"The venison hawk," returned Merrill, picking up a stone.

"Don't throw it, Merrill; he's too beautiful!"

The splendid creature was about the size of the wood-pigeon, but with an air of great wildness and fierceness. He had perched within a rod, where a portion of our dried venison swung, in its tawny richness, in front of the shanty.

---

[1] Lake Champlain was so called by the Iroquois, in honor of Corlear, a Dutchman, and a great favorite, they even designating the governors of New York by his name. Corlear's Lake is the Iroquois term to the present day. The French followers of Champlain in his first encounter, as the leader of the Adirondacks, with the Iroquois on the lake, named it after him.

His color was a brilliant cerulean blue, or rather a glittering steel-blue, with a white head and a savage, red, eager, pitiless eye. It smote like the gleam of a falchion.

"He is after our venison," said Merrill.

"How tame! really like a robin."

"Aha!" said Merrill; "try him! He'd tear your eyes out, and mangle your flesh like a sharp knife, and stab into your very heart with that beak of his, if you'd let him. Why, he's as fierce as a panther, and it's nothing but his savage fearlessness that brings him so close. He'd battle all of us for the partridge or quail that his sharp talons had torn asunder, if we interfered with him. Take care of your eyes, or he'll be at them before you can wink. He's a dangerous creature to be about!"

The bird flew from stump to stump, his bold, sharp eye now fastened upon us, now glancing at the venison, until a well-directed stone from Merrill daunted him away. A flash of blue and white athwart the clearing, and he was gone.

We now started downward, the following lines framing in my brain, with the drizzling rain still falling.

> The hawk he lives as a robber bold!
> He lives but to strike his prey;
> His nest is built on the blasted pine,
> Blasted and jagged and gray!
> He circles and casts his piercing glance
> Down on the woods below;

Woe to the helpless prey that meets
  The eye of the glaring foe!
    Ho, ho, the robber hawk!
      Ho, ho, the robber!
  With his high blue crest and his pitiless breast,
    Ho, ho, the robber!

The hawk he darts from his pine-top throne,
  And skims through his sky-domain;
And the little birds gather and chatter and say,
  "The robber is out again!"
The hawk he sees, and doubles, and darts,
  And sinks, and soars on high;
But the little birds cling to his keen career,
  And strike him from the sky.
    Ho, ho, the robber hawk!
      Ho, ho, the robber!
    No more will his nest hold its savage guest!
      Ho, ho, the robber!

The hawk is an emblem of pitiless kings;
  No matter how wide their power,
They may sway in their terror and might, at last
  Will come the avenging hour!
Gathered together, the trembling weak
  Will grapple the sword and spear,
And the merciless tyrant may tremble and flee,
  But he closes his dread career!
    Ho, ho, the robber hawk!
      Ho, ho, the robber!
    His pitiless strength finds ending at length,
      Ho, ho, the robber!

How bleak and comfortless the shivering woods, shivering in the chill wind! Down, down, down! Down " Hickock's Chuckle," — so I named the slope — slope! — line perpendicular — (within an ace of it!)

I went down by digging my heels in, and sliding down, with my eyes shut, trusting to faith. Hickock went down with four strides and a half, the half scattering a mud puddle all over my blue hunting-shirt.

Down, down, down! At last I concluded to slip all control over my person, and "let it go." I have an indistinct recollection of being wafted down an enormous descent until I heard a rumbling. Was it the White Spirit of the Mountain! No, it was only "The White Ribbon." Pretty nearly down, O tired muscles! At length we reached the stream, and once more we were at our point of departure.

In the cloudy afternoon the guides and I started in the wagon for Scott's. Shortly, I found myself entering the " Whiteface Clove " or " Wilmington Notch."

The mist was ghostly and Ossian-like; the light was spectral; the whole prospect in that weird, half-light, half-dark state. I would not have wondered if I had, like "the son of Morven, standing by the gray stones that marked the graves of his fathers, beheld spirits bending from the mist, and hovering in the wind" (as James G. Brooks, true son of song, the "Florio" of the broken harp, long since gone to the land of the shadow, so finely said), as we entered the north portals. The first time I passed through was on a genial, sunny day in August, when bright lights and dark shadows made splendid the grand picture. But the contrast now! And yet it was the most appropriate of all times to be immersed in the savage sublimity of the gorge. How limitless seemed the height of the soaring and looming walls, mingling with the low, gray mist! Enormous clouds expanded their sable pinions, like swart demons, on the dizzy battlements either side the chasm. And the Ausable — how black, how threatening its wild rapids! Hark! a boom deepening into a stern roar at my right. A leap of flashing waters, contorted into awful frenzy by the bridling rocks! the tameless river cleaving its headlong course downward. "I am the child of the crag and chasm!" the savage stream shouted. "The august Indian Pass is my parent, and I dash and gush and foam downward through the torturing rocks to seek the lake, my home! Ho, ho, how I rush and flash and tumble! Seek to cross my waters — here, here where I pitch like the thunderbolt from the heavens, O catamount of a thousand victories over deer and wild wolf! how I would clutch thy lithe frame and hurl thee to destruction! And even thou, O Whiteface, conqueror of innumerable storms! didst thou think to block my path? Thy crags dare the red-hot lightnings, when the cloud bursts in horrible fury on thy warrior bosom, but thou canst not restrain me, the panther of the torrents.   Behold how I churn wild foam in my wrath !   See how I bound and dash over and through thy puny barriers, flint to the thunder, but pebbles to my rage ! "

The shout continued, but I felt so damp from the mist by this time that I took a drink of whiskey.

Yet truly doth the stream do all it boasts.   The sunshine gleamed out as we left the gorge, as if the golden thing had been frightened from entering, and continued laughing and blinking at us until we reached Scott's.

Glad was I to leave the wagon and stand once more at the green porch of my starting-place ; and, after a delightful dinner, I passed a pleasant afternoon at my most pleasant sojourn.

CHAPTER VI.

SUNDRIES.

Clear Pond. — John Brown's Grave. — Road to Elizabethtown. — Elizabethtown. — Wood-Hill. — The Raven. — Hurricane Peak. — Spot by the Stream. — Sunset. — Night.

THE following morning I started with a guide for Clear Pond, deep in the woods, and distinguished by many as the loveliest water of the forest. It lies toward the Indian Pass, but aside of the trail to it.

From a pasture south of Scott's we struck into the woods, and after crossing a brook (Meadow Brook) by an old log bridge, entered a lumber-road through the forest, with here and there a cleared space. Gradually ascending, a few miles brought us to a dead clearing, the Lower Alger Job, containing a dozen acres. A short distance farther we struck another and much smaller clearing, the Upper Alger Job, with a decayed log-hut, called Nash's Shanty, on its southern side, and on the left of the road. At the end of the Job, and near a second brook which we crossed, the road ceased, and we struck a trail through the woods. At length we came to a third and

broader stream — the south branch of the **West**
Ausable River. We passed over on a prostrate
trunk, and the trail here ceasing, we skirted, by a
line of blazed trees, the east slope of a wild mountain, and descending, saw through the openings of
the woods the glitterings of Clear Pond.

Among the beautiful waters of the wilderness,
this heart-shaped pond is one of the most beautiful.
Sparkling like a gem in its depth of woods, it re-
joices in its loveliness, only for the most part in
behalf of the fauns and dryads. Solitude reigns
generally supreme, broken alone by the fish-hawk,
as he dips his dappled wing for his prey, or the
deer, as it steals to the brink to taste the molten
silver. We had determined to pass the night at
the pond, and the guide began cutting shanty-wood
for the camp-fire, upon a small point which thrust
its tongue out as if to lap the diamond waters.
Sunset found us prepared for the night. And
what a picture the sunset painted! Whereas two
mountains were depicted in Lake Colden, no less
than four found here their photographed features.
To the west, Mount McIntyre was reflected; at
the south frowned Mount Colden; in the east, old
Tahawus painted its black form; while a wooded
mass (the same we had skirted) — tall, save in the
dwarfing presence of these eagle mountains, and
called by me, in default of a better name, "The

Bear," — threw its sable counterfeit at the north.
How beautiful, grand, and impressive ! This little
silver mirror of the woods, scarce a half mile broad
by the same distance in length, holding in its heart
four frowning monsters, — three of them the sublimest of the wilderness, of which one was among
the stateliest in the nation. How like the human
heart enshrining grand objects in its small receptacle, and showing thus its lofty capabilities, as did
Napoleon, —

> " The ebbs and flows of whose single soul
> Were tides to the rest of mankind."

The usual sounds of the forest filled the twilight.
Reverting to the name I had given the mountain,
I wrote the following lines : —

> When Winter with frown puts on his crown,
>   I coil in the hollow trunk !
> And there I doze as the wild wind blows,
>   In my snug, thick garment sunk.
> O there I doze while the snow-drifts close
>   The forests all ghastly chill,
> And the gaunt wolf howls, and the cold cloud scowls
>   On the white and whistling hill.
>
> The hunter I hear come, creaking, near,
>   And I doze the more in my tree ;
> O little I care what death he shall bear
>   So long as he passes by me.
> O little he deems as the keen blast screams,
>   Like pain in the shivering spray,
> That under, the bear coils, free from care,
>   And he treads, unknowing, his way.

Waked from my trance, I start and glance
　At the panther famished and fierce ;
He shrieks as he goes through the choking snows,
　While the bitter hail-arrows pierce.
He shrieks as he goes, for the shy deer knows
　His voice and it flees from the foe ;
But I feed on my fat in my warm, furry mat,
　And the panther may hungry go.

But when comes Spring, and the bluebirds sing,
　And the deep snows melt and run,
I will rouse me then from my darksome den,
　And waddle and pace in the sun.
I will waddle and pace from place to place;
　I will rob of its honey the bee;
I will roam the hollow, in the soft mould wallow,
　And scorn the old caverned tree.

And sometimes nigh to the cabin of Bligh,
　I hate with half fear of his might,
I boldly stray when the hunter's away
　With his hound, his young wifie to fright.
I roll from a bough like a ball ; what a row
　With her screams ! then I rear on my feet ;
I open my jaws, and I dangle my paws,
　And growl, till I, hooting, retreat.

And this hug of mine don't feel like the twine
　Of wifie, O hunter, at home!
With naught but your knife, it is life against life,
　And the chance is — no longer you roam.
A crushed out mass on the trampled grass,
　And a knife, bit and broken, beneath,
Would show the harm of my terrible arm,
　And the cranch of my fearful teeth.

One day I strayed to a berried glade,
　By a thicket I checked my range ;

And a thing I saw with an open jaw, —
   I never saw thing so strange!
And a honeyed scent through the wild wood went,
   And I crept up closer to see ;
I chanced the jaw to touch with my paw,
   And it snapped like a frosty tree.

" Confound the trap! I heard it snap,
   Yet never the bear is there! "
I looked, and nigh was the hunter Bligh,
   But no gun did his shoulder wear.
I reared to my height, but he squared for the fight,
   And his knife flashed keen to the day;
On the berries I'd dined, and I felt not inclined
   For the hug, and I waddled away.

I paced to the hut, and I found it shut,
   For wifie was at the spring;
But the hunter came with his eyes aflame,
   And I fled with my jolting swing.
And all night long, both clear and strong,
   " Hoot, hoot, hunter, hoot! " I cried;
Till the hunter he sprung with his gun, and I flung
   A caper and off I hied.

But his hives I spurned, and the honey I turned
   All down my hungry throat;
Hoot, hoot ! what a time when the sun did climb,
   For wifie sent such a note!
Such a note and squall, and I heard it all,
   And " Hoot, hoot, hoot! " I cried;
Then cantered off, and hushed my scoff
   In a dell by the forest side.

Yes, I tumbled the honey that coined the money,
   I tumbled its soft gold out;
And the bees they stung my short ears and tongue,
   And bit like coals all about.

But what did I care, though my shaggy **hair**
  Was full of the little pests;
I rolled my ball, and I crushed them all
  As I crushed their white diamond-nests.

And thus I go, till the fluttering snow
  Like honey-bees fills the air;
And then I think, as my eyes I wink,
  It is dozing time for the bear!
And then I curl, and then I twirl,
  In the tree till cozy I lie;
And day after day doze on, till the lay
  Of the bluebird sweetens the sky.

I studied the night-scene until my eyes drooped with weariness, and then, having rejected the guide's offer to build a bough-house, threw myself upon a mossy mound as in a downy cradle, and slept. Suddenly the guide, who lay beside me, started to his feet, followed by myself.

" Halloo ! "

The sound was wild and fearful.

" Halloo ! " again repeated.

" Some wanderer in the woods : answer, guide ! "

" Halloo ! " shouted the lad.

" Halloo, halloo, halloo ! " coming nearer and nearer.

" Halloo ! " again, — this time scarce a rod off.

" Here ! " said I ; " here we are ! "

" Halloo ! " with a burst of wild laughter.

" Halloo, halloo ! " ejaculated I ; " we are here ! "

Two fierce eyes glare from the darkness.

" Halloo, halloo, halloo ! " retreating ; " Halloo ! "
and, with another burst of wild laughter, the sounds
ceased.

Who or what the creature was, whether human
or not, I did not know, neither did the guide.
These deep, pathless, unknown woods give birth to
strange sights and strange sounds.

Again we sought the mound, both with feet to
the blazing fire, and I was soon again wandering
in the realm of dreams where —

> " Over its shadowy border glow
> Sweet rays from the world of endless morn."

We left the next morning for Scott's. As the
fine fire of the sunrise lighted upon the four peaks,
methought through the illuminated air they poured
the anthem of their praise to Him, the God of all
things.

Once more through the pleasant woods.

At first the forest presents a tangled mass of un-
dergrowth, mingled with decayed branches dropped
from above, and thrusting their bayonets in all
directions, or crackling to the foot ; with great, prone
trunks mantled in curly moss, scattered every-
where, over a floor of dank, rotten leaves. Round
are pillared, thick as possible, beech, birch, maple,
fir, cedar, spruce, with pines and hemlocks over
all, like lofty intellects over their fellows. Each

10

soars to the light, waving green plumes of foliage
at the top to the currents of air which fail to reach
the depths below.   These depths or vaults are
dark, save where sprinkles of light drain in, or,
here and there, broad streams are poured through
vistas.   Under the lofty trees are others, white-
birch and aspen, with the saplings of the former
trees, and bushes of hopple and sumach, that
scarcely see the light or feel the wind.   But occasionally the tornado tears through, for the sunshine to pierce and the air to circulate.   The tracks
left, time turns into green alleys and dingles, where
the bird builds and the rabbit gambols.   Loosened
trees lean on their fellows, and trees grow on rocks,
grasping them with immense claws which plunge
into the mould below.   Sprouts are rising into
bushes.   Windfalls of prostrate trees lift perpendicular roots.   Upon soft, mossy stumps, saplings
are rooted.   Mossy and lichened ledges are standing around.   Green dells occur where the rill bick-
ers amid water-plants, and hollows are frequent,
through which dashes the shallow rocky streamlet.
All looks monotonous and seems dreary.   But select
a spot.   Let the eye become a little accustomed
to the scene, and how the picturesque beauties,
the delicate, minute charms, the small, overlooked
things steal out, like lurking tints in an old picture.
See that wreath of fern, graceful as the garland of

a Greek victor at the games; how it hides the dark,
crooked root writhing, snake-like, from yon beech!
Look at the beech's instep steeped in moss green
as emerald, with other moss twining round the
silver-spotted trunk in garlands, or in broad, thick,
velvety spots! Behold yonder stump, charred
with the hunter's camp-fire, and glistening, black,
and satin-like in its cracked ebony! See how that
light vine has climbed it, spangling its raven hue
with little leaves! Mark yon mass of creeping
pine mantling the black mould with furzy softness;
view those polished cohosh berries, white as drops
of pearl! See the purple barberries and crimson
clusters of the hopple contrasting their vivid hues;
and that prostrate log, — what Sachem's mantle
ever showed more silken softness and more gorgeous green? while this pyramid of stone-cedar
exhibits a perfect wealth of beautiful fringed em-
broidery, flat as if it had been pressed by enormous
weight, — a sprig of which the most admired
maiden might twist into her purple-black tresses,
and find enhanced their beauty.

And the massive logs, peeled by decay, — what
gray downy smoothness; and the grasses in which
they are weltering, — how full of beautiful motions
and outlines!

And the multitudinous sounds of the woods!
At first all seems silence, breathless quietude. But

sharpen your ears. How the sounds creep out of
their crannies like mice! Hush! the little bell of
the runlet! Flicker, flicker; clap, clap; these are
the flutterings of the white-birch and aspen that
shiver, the delicate things, almost at your look!
Chirp goes the scampering squirrel, the tiny scratch
of his little feet on the dry leaves even audible.
Squall, squall! it is the catbird; and this peevish
screech, — it is the blue jay's. And that low,
solemn harmony, — it is the deep organ of the
pine, mingled with the melody of running water.
Hark, yon hoarse croak! the raven is soliloquizing;
and that loud gabble, — it is the cry of the loon
upon the lake, the cry varied by his clear, triumphal
shout, a hollow, ringing clarion! What a high,
echoing scream! it is that of the black war eagle,
as he launches from the forked top of the dead
pine to scale the cloud and drink the sun-fire.

While passing along, I noticed that grim spectre
of the woods, the raven. He was standing on the
tip-top of a white-pine that swayed with his weight,
eagerly glancing over the wavy expanse of forest
beneath him.

> The raven, he sits on his old gray tree,
>   And he sharpens his sable beak,
> And he glances his keen eye hungrily;
>   O what doth it all bespeak?
> Doth the grim, black sorcerer scent a prey
>   In the billowy wilds below?

Lovely the fresh green realm expands!
　　Do the coverts no victim show?

Bleeding and broken, beneath a crag
　　A helpless hunter lies,
Moaning and struggling and muttering low,
　　And rolling his darkening eyes, —
Moaning and struggling and striving a shout
　　That quivers again to a moan.
O is there none that can bring him aid?
　　O must he there die alone?

In a neighboring cabin there sits a wife,
　　And she sighs in her haunting fear, —
O where is the hunter that left at morn?
　　And she turns to her boy for cheer.
She starts! his footstep is surely without!
　　She opens the door with a bound;
A whine, and a figure leaps up with delight:
　　Joy, joy, 'tis the long lost hound!

She sees not the raven, but there he sits;
　　His beak is sharpened and keen;
He croaks, " Now surely the hunter is dead! "
　　And he eagerly floats to the scene.
But still the hunter, he wearily moans,
　　And this is his sorrowful moan,
O is there none that can bring him aid?
　　O must he there die alone!

A rustle, — he looks; he gazes and shakes!
　　The raven, the raven he sees!
With hungry eye and with pointed beak,
　　As he lights on the neighboring trees.
O horrible thought! is he then the prey
　　Of the raven so deadly and grim?
He struggles and moans and he strives to rise,
　　With his eyeballs sunken and dim.

But hearken! his hound's voice! the sorcerer flies
    With a croak like a demon in pain!
A form bends over, — his wife! his wife!
    And hope glows within him again.
His wife and boy with their blended strength
    Uplift the poor hunter; away
They bear their dear burden, hark! not the croak!
    But the robin's clear, hopeful lay!

We reached Scott's, and in the forenoon I left on foot to visit the famous John Brown's grave, two miles distant on the road to the Lower Saranac Lake. It lies a half-mile to the south of the road at the summit of a bluff two hundred feet above the West Ausable, that winds black and rocky through the glen below.

I passed a settlement in the hollow, and, ascending, entered a pair of bars. A rough track through woods and new fields soon brought me to a clearing where Brown's former dwelling, a low, unpainted, board structure, stood on the farther edge. It is now occupied by another family, and in the plainly furnished sitting room are portraits, stern, white-haired, and white-bearded, of the Harper's Ferry leader.

A large boulder stands in front of the house, and beneath it a dark slab of coarse marble, in a little inclosure, marks the spot where John Brown rests. The slab was originally over the remains of his grandfather, but it was removed from New England by Brown's particular directions and placed over his own ashes.

The following are the inscriptions, taken on the spot : —

The front of the slab runs thus : " In Memory of Captn John Brown Who Died at New York Septr ye 3. 1776 in the 48 year of his age.

" John Brown Born May 9, 1800, was Executed at Charlestown Va. Dec. 2, 1859.

" Oliver Brown Born May 9, 1839, was killed at Harper's Ferry, Oct 17, 1859."

The reverse of the slab shows the following : —

" In memory of Frederick son of John and Dianthe Brown — born Dec 21, 1830, and murdered at Osowotome Kansas, Aug 30, 1856, for his adherence to the cause of freedom.

" Watson Brown Born Oct 7, 1835, was wounded at Harper's Ferry Oct 17 and died Oct 19, 1859."

On the boulder was engraved, in enormous letters : —

" John Brown
1859."

Although the slab records the inscriptions, the remains of John Brown himself only here repose, with grass and wild flowers covering his grave.

I ascended the boulder, and immediately the puny slab vanished from my eyes, for on the north towered Old Whiteface, and south soared the great Tahawus. Truly two grand grave-stones (accidental, of course, but none the less striking and poetic), between which John Brown sleeps, reared in everlasting rock by the Great God himself.

I heard a great deal concerning Brown from the neighbors about. They all, friends and foes, bore testimony to his native dignity of mind, person, and manner. He was tall and gaunt, reserved in speech, but kindly. While conversing with any one, he would draw out all that one knew, disclosing little himself.

Inflexible in purpose, and unconquerable in spirit, Nature seemed to have cast him in the iron mould of the Puritan warrior.

Many scenes of his wild and stormy life were romantic and remarkable.

What more touching picture to those who broke into the Engine House in the gray dawn which saw him a prisoner, than John Brown, kneeling, his rifle in his right hand, his left on the pulse of his dying boy shot by his side, while another of his sons lay dead at his feet. The father and the warrior! bowed in his anguish, yet with front to the foe; his eye drooping in unfathomable grief, yet flashing with a soldier's courage!

Striking, diagonally across the clearing, I descended the steep slope by a path to the Ausable, which I crossed on its bed of rocks. I looked back after regaining the highway. There stood the dwelling, lifted above the surrounding landscape, — an object visible about for a considerable distance.

The next day I passed entirely at Scott's, noting the little scenes and incidents of the secluded spot. At sunrise, the whole landscape was shrouded in mist. No one could have imagined that all the tall crests of the Adirondacks were around.

" Why, Jake (Mr. Scott's nephew), there's Lake Placid ! I had no idea the lake could be seen from this point ! "

Jake looks and smiles.

" I haven't any idea now of it."

" But there it is ! right over the meadow ! "

It lay a perfect picture, with points and headlands. Jake smiles again.

" There's the breakfast-bell, sir ! After breakfast, where's your lake ? "

Sure enough where was it ? Lifted bodily into the trees, by the sun ; nothing left but a fragment or two of the mist that made it.

But the mountains — they were visible, particularly McIntyre, south, and Whiteface, north, from base to summit.

Of all the Adirondack crests, Tahawus is not only the tallest and sublimest, but the most beautiful. Nothing can exceed the gracefulness with which it slopes from its tapering top to its spacious base. And Whiteface is next in grace as well as grandeur, with form nearly similar. Mount McIntyre stands boldly out from Scott's door-step with a rather regular slope, ploughed deeply with its ravines, like an old man's face with wrinkles, adding to its rugged stateliness.

Mount Colden next (to repeat this limning of Scott's mountain-girdle) uplifts its hump-back shape, devoid of beauty. Next the Tahawus Pyramid, rise at the southeast the Dial and Dix's Peak. The latter, viewed from Mud Pond, stretches its savage length, with naught but terror. But the Dial from the same point! Of all misshapen monsters, this mountain is the most misshapen. Beauty is as foreign to it as to a wolf. Completing the mountain zone, at the east stand the Keene Range in rounded billows, and then Whiteface; at the southwest glimmer the pinnacles of Mount Seward; and south, rounding like a loon's breast, close to the west slope of McIntyre (with the Indian Pass between), and running thence northwest, is seen Wallface.

Eleven o'clock and Jake " hitches the ox-team " to the stone-boat, and starts to the neighboring field to fill the hogshead, standing by the house, with the only water the family uses.

This little incident over, dinner (and a good one) comes. Then Jake splits a log or two, or starts for the barn, or " Uncle Scott " and he hold high confab on affairs of the farm. Then the afternoon, then tea, then night — and then — bedward.

The following day, after bidding adieu to honest, kindly Mr. Scott, and that truly Christian woman his wife, I left in a private two-horse wagon, for Elizabethtown, to carry out my plan of visiting the magnificent gorge of the Dial.

Soon after leaving Scott's pleasant plateau, we began to ascend. The forest advanced close to the road, but at the south I saw pinnacles rising two thousand feet, — the Keene Range, into which we had now entered. The narrow road grew miry, rough, and channeled by the brooklets of the Range. At either side the mountain we were ascending, covered with woods, rose almost perpendicularly. After considerable toil, our horses mastered the ascent (Chimney Hill), where the gorge through which the road ran afforded only room for the track. At the north towered the wall of the mountain, while opposite fell a steep ravine through which the vision pierced to a distant glitter of Lake Champlain. Down we then dipped in our steep, stony, furrowed descent. Still frowned the southern pinnacles, wooded to the top, and still towered the mountain from the edge of the road on the north. Down one of the loftiest and wildest of the pinnacles in full view at our right, scowled a jagged, broken, ghastly streak, the track of a slide, tearing to the quick of its granite muscles the mountain's flesh, and hurling tree and rock beneath in its irresistible and awful course. A waterfall now sprang and foamed through the terrific cleft, filling but half the channel, and the low rumble of its path touched my ear.

At last we emerged upon level ground. The mountains, either side, wheeled to the horizon, leaving a broad, open landscape, showing fields of grain and pasture lots, with kine grazing and flocks nibbling. It was Alsted's, or Heald Hill. Merrily whirled our wheels over the smooth, hard, road, — I catching a rearward glimpse of a blue chaos of mountains rolling upon the plateau over which we were speeding. Homesteads thickened in rough fields either side, or among apple-orchards, grain-fields, and meadows; occasionally a pedestrian, or a wagon, or the red box of the peddler, went past; all betokening that we were leaving the forest for rural life. A half score of miles brought us to the village of Keene. I have noticed before the terrible freshet which visited this place. It occurred ten years ago, from a series of water-spouts bursting on the steep water-shed of the region and toward Elizabethtown; also by the breaking away of the State Dam at the foot of the Lower Ausable Pond. In the quiet and seeming security of midnight, a roaring broke upon the slumbers of the village people. Rushing into the open air, they saw the horrible flood, flashing and tumbling full upon them with the roaring of blended thunders. Dwellings were swept away like straws, and even the aged and the sick felt the chill waters piling upon them and perished.

" 'Twas a dreadful bad time on't," said my driver. " To be woke up in the middle of the night whiles making a sleep on't, and finding yourself agoin' full split to Davy's Locker."

" How many were lost ? " asked I.

" Two sarten, ef not three ! A sick gal and her grandmum, and I bleeve an old feller with the rheumatiz. At all events, he never was seen afterwards. Some folks said he cut stick to Californy, but I bleeve he cut stick to t'other world, on top o' this onmarciful frash. That's it — whew ! But I say, squire ! there's awful good rum in this store. Rael Santa Cruz ! " smacking his lips.

We paused at the store and I gave the man a glass of the white liquor, after his eloquent funeral oration on the death of the poor old man, and then glanced around. Wrappers and folds of woolens and dry goods were at one side ; hardware and crockery on the other; and cheeses, firkins of butter, hams, eggs, barrels of mackerel, and hogsheads on their stomachs in the dim background, — with a rough counter round the whole ; while tin pans, wooden pails, curry-combs, whips, and lanterns, dangled from the rough rafters above.

We pursued our way.   Partridge or Spruce Hill
was our next ascent of any moment.   It wound
upward for two miles.   Turning my head accidentally, a most grand prospect, even in this enchanted
region of grand prospects, broke upon me.   There
surged the Keene Mountains, rolling gigantic billows
in softest, sweetest azure upon the valley, like those
of an ocean that might whelm the world.   The
standing forth of the peak of Tahawus on the ascent from the side of Lake Colden, was scarce finer
in effect.

How the road could have twisted and turned so
as to escape the spurs of these granite masses I do
not understand, but the traveller scarcely notices
the mountains while traversing the track.

As a turn hid the prospect, a curtain seemed
dropped between me and those mountain glories in
which I had so long reveled.   But I cherished
their remembrance ; for as travellers in the Orient
secrete gems in their flesh against the time of need,
so do we enshrine precious memories in our hearts,
to brighten life when darkened by calamity or deso-
lated by sorrow.

Attaining the crest, we rolled down the descent
on whirring wheels, striking fire frequently from
the flinty road.   The wooded acclivities either side
continually shifted their outlines, presenting manifold shapes, — now pyramids, now truncated cones,

now sea-like surges. Mile after mile jogged away, and I was fancying wild Tahawus struggling in the coils of a savage snow-storm, when my dream was broken by the voice of the driver.

"Here's another slide, and a big one 'twas!" said he, pointing to a deep, pallid cut on the steep mountain side at the right.

It must, indeed, have been terrible. Trees crushed under enormous rocks, rocks fractured into stones, stones ground into pebbles, pebbles mashed into dust, filled the eye with awful chaos. At the foot of the declivity, the launched thunderbolt had completely altered the channel of a stream, so that it described a huge half-circle, cutting a "monstrous cantle" out of its former border.

We now struck the Boquet River, the stream of this portion of the region, as the Ausable is of the one below.

Shortly afterwards, we came to a most singular looking crag, impending over the track.

"What is that up there, driver?" I asked. It looked like an enormous elephant, or rather a mammoth, about to jump.

"That!" said the driver looking up so as to draw his mouth and eyes down like a boy's squash-lantern. "Why, that's Little Pitch-Off! Big Pitch-Off stands out here at Edmunds' Ponds."

The wonder is, that Little Pitch-Off sticks on at

all. It seems as if a breath might loosen it; but it is picturesque, and appears to grin at the terror it inspires in those passing beneath.

We reached Elizabethtown at sunset. This little mountain village is one of the most striking and romantic in the State. Hemmed in by towering peaks, away from railroads and travel, eight miles east of Lake Champlain, with merely a rough, stony road for the link between, — it is scarcely known to the rest of the world. It contains, perhaps, five hundred inhabitants, occupies a portion of a high plateau and the plain beneath, and is the capital of Essex County. On the plateau stand the Court-house, with the County Clerk's office by its side, two churches, and several rural dwellings, some very pleasant, with trees and grassy court-yards. On the plain, northward, are manifold dwellings, with several stores along the main street, which stripes the plateau as well, — and also on the two or three lateral streets.

I drove to the " Valley House," an inn at the foot of the plateau and the centre of the village. There I sojourned several days, exploring the hamlet and its surroundings.

A beautiful, cultivated gorge opens the plateau at the north, leading to " Rice's Falls," a wild, tumbling cascade. The gorge is traversed by " The Branch," an arm of the Boquet. Rural and beautiful it looks in the low light of the evening, when a film trembles over the plateau, and a fine sheen kindles the peaks around it. How green the gold-lighted grass, how bright the trees, how pleasant the homesteads!

The Raven, Wood Hill, and the Cobble, are the summits of the village. A few miles distant stands Hurricane Peak, and still farther on Saddleback.

Wood Hill overlooks the plain. Its ascent is not long, but steep; an elongation of " Hickock's Chuckle."

The view is beautiful. On the left gleams the Branch, leading into the main valley of the Boquet River. Far to the right smiles the lovely vale of Keene, with its mountain range, and Little Pitch-Off impending. The Pleasant Valley (for by that name was Elizabethtown known to the early settlers — or rather " The Valley," as it is still called by the country people) lies dotting its plateau and plain. At the extreme left of the charming picture glows the Boquet Valley, with mountain-tops at its side and in front, seeming, at the distance of several miles, to block the valley into a *cul de sac*. Only in appearance, though, for it winds to the famous Split Rock, a cataract of the Boquet. The scene well repays for all the toil of the ascent.

The Raven (also overlooking the plain) was my

11

next point. Its ascent was comparatively easy, although it is the highest (two thousand feet) of the immediate Elizabethtown Peaks. The picture below is the same as Wood Hill, only on a more extended scale. The only noticeable feature I saw on the mountain, was a tremendous hollow at the northeast side, near the crest, formed by some convulsion of nature. A tornado, from appearances, had dashed against it, and twisted the tough cedars so that they seemed as if wishing to scud for protection into the hollow's depths.

It took me an hour to climb the acclivity; I was just fifteen minutes in coming down. My legs took it upon themselves to run off with me, and they had it all their own way. I have an indistinct recollection of pitching downward in a series of convulsive bounds, which might have been summersets for aught I remember. In fact, I thought myself turned into a gyrating wheel, and it was only when my runaway legs deposited me safe and sound at the foot, although perfectly breathless, that I saw I was down. I'm inclined to think, sometimes, I was pitched down like a crowbar by the wrathful Raven, in behalf of the brother peaks I had invaded.

The Cobble (a perpendicular pocket edition of the Dial, bearing a similar dome — a chaos of gray rocks — a mountain huddled into its bones), overlooked the plateau, and I thought until my foot should be flapped like the fly's, it might overlook it forever before I went up it.

Hurricane Peak I did ascend with a party. It showed the usual waterfall, with the mantle of forest to the neck, and bare, rocky head. There was no trail, and right glad was I when the ascent was accomplished. It put me in mind of the Scripture question, " What went ye out in the wilderness for to see ? A reed shaken with the wind?" No, but a crest shaken (nearly) with a whirlwind. Most appropriately named is that peak. The wind fairly poured a torrent over it. I have an indistinct recollection of dim shapes and fluttering garments huddling together for mutual protection from the wolfish blasts, while I clutched the rim of my hat with the clutch of desperation.

But the view was superb. On the north, Whiteface, with a savage stretch of wilderness between ; west, McIntyre and Colden, and Tahawus the Titan ; then the Gothics, pinnacled like thunder-caps, with the dark, wild ravine of the Ausable Ponds between them and the Dial, which frowned in close neighborhood to Dix's Peak.

At the south, that film of mist ! Mount Pharaoh, the Black Mountain of the Indian, where, in the old time, flashed knife and tomahawk of Mohawk and Adirondack in deadly strife !

To the east, that long, broad, crystal painting!
Lake Champlain! "The Open Gate" of the Iroquois — with crossing sails and gliding steamboats,
and the light-house on its point — with its bays
and headlands, and its magnificent background, the
Green Mountains of Vermont, domed with Mount
Mansfield, — "The Old Man of the Mountains,"
and the Camel's Hump, — "The Lion Couchant"
of the French.

Beneath shone the Elizabethtown Valley, and
southward stretched the scenic beauty of New
Russia, with woodlands and waters, fields and
homesteads.

I studied the sunset picture intently, and then,
with it glowing like a star in my brain, joined the
party in the descent.

We had the customary picnic at the base of the
waterfall, with the red, evening light sprinkled
like fireflies about the rocky dingle, and the basin
of the fall, reflecting our crimson spot of fire, and
the picnic things scattered upon its rim, until it
shone like a cabinet painting; and then through the
beautiful gold twilight accomplished our return, four
miles, to the village.

One of my haunts was The Branch. Many an
hour have I whiled away in a picturesque spot close
at the brink of the bright waters, just below the
store at the bridge, with a grassy lawn opposite.

There was a pool, formed by a little board dam and two or three water plants. In this pool was a little whirlpool, and it drew in all the leaves and sticks floating downward. A bee came struggling along the little sparkling current, half drowned. A leaf was twirling in the mouth of the whirlpool. The bee was wafted to, and tumbled upon it, his gold-banded body gleaming like a dot of stray sunshine. He rested a moment, wiped his wings with his black velvet legs, and was off.

The leaves drawn down would twist and vanish under the dam. In the whirlpool was a little fleet of dotted water-flies, with a dozen fierce, black pirate iron-clads of skating spiders jerking hither and yon as if to pick up, one by one, the flies.

I have watched this little by-show by the hour; then back I would go to the tavern.

Sunset. A broad beam bathes Wood Hill and gilds the pretty white porch opposite the " Valley House." A ray then shoots off toward the red brick mansion of Judge Hand, standing in its court-yard in the midst of patriarchal trees, looking on The Branch opposite the tavern. West, the lustre turns into a street of gold, " Water Street," leading past handsome dwellings among trees up toward the domicile of Doctor Hale, nestling in foliage, with a lovely ribbon of a stream at the rear.

Then it tinges at the bridge the visitant Underhill, poet and humorist; and bathes Gifford and McEntee, Huntington and Hubbard, under the pleasant trees of The Branch, by the tavern-porch. How the canvas of these artists will glow in the future with the gems of this almost untouched region which Art is just beginning to explore!

And now for the plateau. Over the bridge, up the board walk, and what a beautiful picture! A horizon of peaks, each peak a gigantic violet or a vision of rose purple. How bright the gorge, while even the Cobble smiles. Ah, there is Hurricane Peak, seeming as soft and peaceful as an infant's eye. And now twilight falls, and the plateau begins to glimmer as if seen through slightly smoke-tinged glass. Objects loom; dwellings, trees, horses, wagons, and wandering kine. And at last, Night, with her starry purple —

"How beautiful is Night!"

It is the season of thought, of retrospection, as the day is of action and anticipation. It is consecrated to memory, to holy wishes, to lofty aspirations. It is the period of serene tranquillity, of healing quiet, of consoling rest.

Day distracts us: we are ever bracing our energies to life's battle; our heart is a sentry always guarding against expected change; our mental eye on the alert for probable calamity.

Talk of the battle-field which lasts a few, brief

hours ! Life's battle is never ended, and though the crimson field be heaped with dead, how many thousand broken hearts attest the awfulness of that struggle which clings to us throughout our pathway.

But night brings a pause even in that conflict. A divine peace hallows it ; the darkness is blessed. Faces of the 'old time rise, voices of the old time sound : we look, we listen, and are happy.

And as day is akin to joy, so is night to sorrow. And yet a tender sorrow, born of pure, and, it may be, repentant thought. By day, with its cares, anxieties, and hurrying efforts, we do not see life in all its solemnities, its duties, its dignity, its mystery, its momentous interests, its tremendous responsibilities. But night, with its calmness and peace, unfolds them to us, as it unfolds the stars that daylight hides.

Ah, the musings that night has only witnessed ! Ah, the struggling resolves, the remorseful pangs, the penitential tears !

And what tenderness have the stars seen, and what vows of love have been whispered in the ear of the beautiful moon !

Yes, truly is life akin to grief ; — and how necessary is it to our nature ! As the light consumes the inanimate substances it rests upon, so that it requires the night to restore what is lost during the day, thus does prosperity batten upon what is best within us, only to be restored by the dark blessing of sorrow.

And faith, the guide, consoler, comforter! How it rises in the night's purifying and sustaining hours! And how it lifts our natures toward God, as the blossoms of the moosewood are lifted to its summit by the light of the blessed sun!

CHAPTER VII.

THE GORGE OF THE DIAL.

THE time had now arrived for my departure to seek the Dial Gorge. On the eve of it, however, I was doomed to disappointment. Elijah Simons, the most noted and trustworthy hunter and trapper of the region, was taken sick. He it was who had originated my desire to visit the spot. He, with the exception of his brother William, the host of the "Valley House," and a keen hunter himself, had been the only visitor to the gorge, and was perfectly familiar with its locality.

No present prospect of Elijah's recovery showed itself, and at last, with two guides hired for the occasion, I started with Homer Martin (one of our most promising young landscape artists, who was painting in the region) and my son, for the long desired point, armed with full instructions from Elijah.

Our first destination was Russell Root's, twenty-three miles distant, over a good road and through the beautiful scenery of New Russia. Midway, I was startled by the great bulk of Dix's Peak, soaring into the clouds at our right, with Macomb's Mountain below, together with "The Giant of the Valley" (or "The Dome") and Bald Mountain. We passed the Dead Water, an expansion of the Schroon (the east branch of the Hudson), whose source lies in New Pond, farther north, and is also connected with ponds at the east and west. At the Dead Water extensive Iron Works are situated. We passed also North Hudson, a cluster of houses, and at sundown arrived at Root's, a white two-story tavern at the intersection of two roads, with cleared fields around and mountain-tops in the distance. One of these roads leads to the beautiful Upper Works, thirty miles distant, over a corduroy that shakes the bones at the bare mention of the word. The few people living on the route, according to report, have the corduroy ague. Even the trees quiver as if earthquakes were there dancing. Only a wagon whose axles would defy a thunderbolt, could withstand these broken corduroys a mile.

The next morning, I was awakened by the tinkle of the anvil from the red blacksmith-shop opposite. Sallying out, I heard next the pleasant sound of the carpenter's saw, from the shop below, — for quite a settlement has the industrious and enterprising Root gathered around him. Standing on his porch, one realizes how his persistent energy has triumphed over nature. A sign-post also salutes the eye, standing before the tavern, surmounted by an enormous pair of moose antlers, with " Russell Root's Inn " lettered on their broad flat surfaces.

There is a lovely glimpse of field and woodland at the left of the porch, and a graceful wheel of the road, leading past the blacksmith-shop to Crown Point, on Lake Champlain.

The other road leads from Elizabethtown, and passes by Root's, to Schroon and Lake George.

Early and bright the following morning we left for our goal. As before remarked, the Gorge is almost totally unknown even in its own neighborhood. Accordingly I felt the excitement of one about to see an undiscovered wonder. It lies completely out of the trail either of hunter or trapper, buried in the fastnesses of two savage mountains, the least known among the ranges. And then, its magnificence, looming from Elijah's statements, heated my enthusiasm to boiling point.

We traversed the highway, with the west branch of the Schroon River dashing at the south through wild woods, five miles to Fenton's Tavern, a quiet spot of many picturesque capabilities ; thence struck in a northeasterly direction a rough road, ascending widely cleared heights, whence lay a broad forest landscape, with Schroon Mountain — the Spirit Mountain of the red man—lifting its dial-top grandly at the south, and then through twining woods. This road we travelled for three miles, and came to Clear Pond, a pretty sheet, a mile long and half a mile wide, with no islands. There is quite a farm cleared at the pond, but I looked in vain for the customary homestead.

The west branch of the Schroon, or Sturdevant's Branch, is born in the gorge of the Dial, and runs into Mud Pond. Thence it issues and flows by the west side of Clear Pond, to which it is linked by the outlet of the pond, a quarter of a mile long.

We reached the head of the pond, and then commenced the frown of Fortune. Hitherto all had been easy and clear, but the guides were, as well as ourselves, in an unknown region. And here let me remark, that not a particle of blame justly attaches to the guides for the ill-luck that clung to us the rest of the trip. They did all that experienced woodmen could do, but they could not perform impossibilities, that is, scent out the trail as the hound scents the deer.

On reaching the head of the pond, we should have turned at our left, and would then have found a good path (nay, a veritable lumber road) leading directly to Mud Pond, the next point on our way. But the screen of forest hid it, and it was passed. Rounding the pond we arrived at its foot, and here we searched for the road that I knew from Elijah's instructions existed. But no road leading in the supposed direction of Mud Pond was found. A score of times we essayed some opening in the woods, some cleft in the foliage, some broken path, some natural vista, some narrow dingle. The prostrate trunk led us onward a little way, to disappoint us at last; the opening was soon blocked, the cleft soon closed, the broken path became more broken, the vista quickly vanished, the dingle became lost. Etchings of roads indeed lay about, but they only led to some chopping, and then ceased. We became thus aware that the pond had been a lumbering point; consequently its shores were filled with these " signs," and we abandoned them at once.

At length a path at the foot of the pond did present itself. How green and open and pleasant the little vista looked, inviting the step with an irresistible charm ! And we entered. A sunny knoll was crossed, and we all congratulated ourselves that our troubles were over. Soon would the blue gleam of Mud Pond shine through the trees; and on we went. But the path began dwindling to a trail, and faint at that; broken corduroys over marshy spots became frequent. Wilder and wilder the trail grew; prostrate trees blocked, thickets covered it. The choking foliage twined at length so densely, that the broken spots in the mouldering corduroys could not be seen. And thus our progress became slow and painful. At last all traces of the track ceased in a tangled " wind slash." The thick blackberry vines stung and mangled us; the broken logs of the corduroy threatened every instant dislocation of our limbs. But on we went. I felt confident we were lost, still I struggled forward, dashing the thickets aside to see where I could plant my feet in safety.

At length sunset began to filter through the western leaves — and then twilight to darken the woods. At our right hills arose, but what range no one knew. They looked threateningly at us for daring the depths of the forest without knowledge of our way. At last we came to a brook (Niagara Brook, as we on our return to Root's discovered), flowing in the direction of Clear Pond. We left it and struggled along our blind way, openings in the woods and bits of broken corduroy alone telling us we were still upon a road. But as the rainy dark fell, we came to (as we thought) another brook. It ran in an entirely different direction from the first, and the guides ordered a halt. Indeed, it was time, for the woods were now so dark, it was impossible to proceed. A

penetrating rain, began falling, and there, by the
mysterious brook (Niagara Brook, as we subsequently learned, deflected), we made our most comfortless bivouac. India-rubber blankets stretched
on the reeking ground protected our chilled limbs,
and the camp-fire warmed them, but everything else
was disheartening and disagreeable. And so the
weary night passed, and the pallid morning came.
Our return to Clear Pond was determined on; we
retraced our painful path, and reached the pond
after sore fatigue. We afterward ascertained that
the trail we had so painfully trod, was the Point
Cedar Road — an old track abandoned for twenty
years to the panthers and wolves, but in other days
intersecting, westward from a point on the Elizabethtown Road, the route to the Upper Works.

We passed the afternoon at the pond. Finding
a raft in the shallows, some of us propelled it into
the middle of the expanse. And lo! up started
Dix's Peak, the Dial, and Macomb's Mountain,
toward the north; as if to invite us. A low, wild
hill stretched thitherward, offering a comparatively
open ridge. Sunset came, and with it a tremendous caterwauling among a small family of loons,
which had at last succeeded in rising from the
pond. Three times did they circle the water in
their flight, each time nearer to us, as if demanding
why we had intruded on their realm, until, with a

series of discordant laments, they vanished over a ridge to reach, probably, some wilder water. At night we crept under a slanting roof of boards, left by some frequenter of the pond, and I, for one, listened to the intermittent patter of the rain all night. Occasionally I looked out. A burst of moonlight would brighten the pond and woods, touch the top of Mount Pharaoh with a glitter of silver, or open on the brow of Schroon Mountain in a glance of white, but again the scene would blacken and the rain fall. The morning at last came, bright and beautiful. With risen spirits and renovated strength, we started for our conducting ridge, despairing of finding Elijah's wood-road. O the horrors of that three-mile tramp!

I cannot describe in detail, for my memory is but a chaos of floundering, desperate, awful efforts. The forest twined its net so closely, the eye was debarred from more than a foot's sight in any direction, while the feet were clogged as with manacles by the tough, clinging underbrush. We fought the forest hand to hand up the acclivity, to find but a rough path at best, leading us through blinding thickets, until at last the welcome gleam of water broke from far below. This could only be Mud Pond, and so it turned out to be. We ploughed boldly downward, and at last, with my limbs aching from the terrific exertion I had put forth, I stood with the others upon the margin of the pond. Blue as heaven it shone, with one island midway; and the Dial, Dix's Peak, and Macomb's Mountain in front and east, while west waved the Boreas summits. Before us we saw the rounding of the Dial and the Peak, forming the Gorge, almost identical with that of McIntyre and Wallface from Scott's, shaping the Indian Pass. A splendid mountain picture indeed.

On the brink I found an old mink-trap — doubtless set there by Elijah. A wild poplar sprout had taken possession of the boxing, and the spindle was thrust like a dark dart through a plume of fern.

An hour was passed by the guides in building a raft, and on it we were wafted to the leafy island. There we spent the remainder of the day, and watched the pond changing color in the sunset. Then came the night. I knew I was in the wildest heart of the wild mountain-region, and was pleased with the mystery. But on the whole I rather wished myself back to civilization, and for the first time. At night I stepped with my guides to the shore of the island, and looked out upon the black landscape. Gloomy masses told the mountains, and they seemed close at hand. Profound stillness prevailed. Suddenly two reports rang; my guides had fired their rifles for the echo — and a splendid echo was awakened. It ran round the

12

shores in reduplications; it seemed as if from every point a rattling explosion rebounded. Macomb's Mountain tossed the sound to Dix's Peak, which sent it to the Dial: that in turn hurled it to the Boreas crests.

Shortly after we stretched ourselves on the moss of our island bivouac, close to our camp-fire, but in vain I wooed slumber to my weary eyelids. I dwelt on the contrast between our comfortless couch upon the damp moss, with the trees only for roof, and the warm, dry, cosy shanty.

Against the rough and wrinkled rock
   The little forest shanty leans;
The spruce and tamarack interlock,
   And one tall pine the doorway screens,
   Through which the hut its radiance gleans.

Lithe, slender poles its rafters form;
   The walls are wrought of cedar rind;
Within spreads shelter cool or warm;
   The creeping rains no cranny find,
   Nor prying snow, nor prowling wind.

Torch of the pine its sunshine makes;
   Sprays of the spruce its couches pile;
When into stars the sunset breaks,
   Away the hours the hunters while,
   Then up with morning's earliest smile!

Rich sassafras and spicy birch
   With cool airs scent the brightening gloom;
And as the rich, red sunbeams search
   For sheen of birds and brooks and bloom,
   How lightsome looks the little room!

There stands the rod, and there the gun;
　The brazen reel gives meteor blink;
Piles of bright trout flash back the sun,
　　While dangling hang in sylvan link
　　The black-cat dark and ruddy mink.

Stares on the stump the venison's head;
　The antlers crown another by;
Deftly the dainty limbs are shred;
　　The fresh-drawn pelt lies, careless, nigh,
　　While looks the hound with longing eye.

The camp-fire nightly burns before;
　Heaped bullets glance a leaden tint;
Red shirts, blue blankets, patch the floor;
　　Tangles of sapphire fish-hooks glint;
　　Neck-yoke and net strange shadows print.

And round the fire the hunters sit,
　Bright in the broad and flickering blaze;
From lip to lip talk's pinions flit,
　　Or thought on homeward journey strays,
　　While tower the trees in glittering glaze.

Morn! hark, hurrah! that bugle clear!
　It is, it is the exultant hound!
Now faintly far, now loudly near!
　　Comes in the air the ringing sound,
　　As if Joy's self his trumpet wound.

Grasp rifle — off — the run-way seek!
　Hide in the ambush-saplings swift!
Hark, a nigh pattering! like a streak
　　A form, where these fir-branches lift,
　　Glances behind that tree-top drift.

It comes, it comes! it is the deer
　With shouldered antlers; — on he skims;

Once more the hound sends echoing cheer;
    A shot — he drops with quivering limbs,
    And swift a crimson current swims.

The wood-knife flashes at his throat,
    And lifeless now the victim lies;
Hurrah, hurrah! sound loudest note!
    Hurrah, hurrah, the noble prize
    Is ours! and thus time, glittering, flies.

O priceless memories! peerless days!
    Pinioned with flowers, O forest-life!
Oft will my lyre in gladness raise
    Song to those shades with rapture rife,
    Far from the world's wild, weary strife!

O priceless memories! peerless days!
    Shrined in pure joys your scenes I see!
And in my rude and rapid lays
    The willing wings of fancy flee
To where the wilds I tread, happy at heart and free.

About midnight I awoke, and found a dreadful storm raging, — the shores (as in the case of the rifle-shots) firing off reports to each crash of the thunder, and leaping into convulsive life at every glance of the lightning. The Lion of Dix's Peak bounded forth with a roar; the Dial started out with a grand look of rage; Macomb's Mountain reeled in a witch's dance at the rapid flashes; the Boreas tossed the keen darts from crest to crest; while the foaming Pond shouted to the blasts, and glared in the fierce torches of the clouds. It was altogether a fearful scene, this battle of the ele-

ments, and in the heart of the Adirondack soli-
tudes.

The next morning dawned warm and cloudless,
and revealed the three terrific slides that gash
the north flank of Dix's Peak. They made me
shudder to see them — spent thunderbolts now,
but how fearful at the time of their launching!

I went to the island's edge, and, over the blue,
rippling water, looked at the point of the savage
hill opposite, and the wild ridge beyond covered
with black, scowling, threatening woods, through
which lay my course to the Gorge. I knew the
whole course was pathless; and that it was most
formidable even Elijah's reticent description plainly
showed, hardy hunter and trapper that he was,
and despising the stern hardships of the forest.
My fatigues of the last day or two had been enormous and most exhaustive. They had told se-
verely upon my strength. Neither my guides, my
companions, nor myself had the slightest knowledge
personally of those intervening woods, stretching
away, as if in defiance, from the head of the pond
to the rounding down of the tremendous mountains
that betrayed the lair of the lurking Gorge. And
so, with a vivid recollection of the hardships and
sufferings encountered in our coming, and an unpleasant apprehension of trouble to come in our
returning, and after a consultation with my com-

panions, the idea of attempting a visit to the Gorge,
at all events for the present, was regretfully abandoned:

—— " rather bear the ills we have
Than fly to others that we know not of; "

and so we acted. Again we deposited ourselves
upon the raft, which bore us safely back to the main
shore, and then pushed into the woods, on our return path. All the horrors of the preceding day
were reënacted, and all the fatigues renewed.
How gladdened I was when the bright blue mirror
of Clear Pond flashed upon my eye, I need scarcely
mention; and with buoyant step I trod with my
companions and the guides the plain open road that
led to Fenton's, around whose board we enjoyed a
plentiful repast.

Subsequently I drew from the taciturn Elijah a
circumstantial account of the spot on his first visit
to it. Even from his matter of fact descriptions, it
was plain to be seen that a fearfully sublime and
most magnificent gorge exists, between the Dial
and its stately neighbor Dix's Peak, almost entirely
unknown to the present day.

A trapping excursion one autumn had brought
him to Mud Pond. Seeing the opening between
the mountains, he was seized with a desire to know
what existed there, supposing from the " lay of the
land " that it must be a gorge. Finding a boat

he floated up to the head of the pond and struck into the woods. There was no trail, and no indication either in blazed tree or in trap that human foot had trodden there before him. He crossed the intervening point and ridge, and for three long miles he battled the forest, gradually ascending. At the end of the three miles, the ground became more abrupt. Up, up (as in the case of the Indian Pass) he went, higher and higher, his expectations rising with every footfall, until a half mile was passed. It then became a steep break-neck ascent. Upward he clambered, clutching branch, rock, and sapling. For twenty or thirty rods he thus dragged himself, when suddenly he reached level ground.

What was the towering thing at his left, soaring close from his feet up, dizzily up, until it seemed to clutch the heavens. It was a terrific wall, a horrible precipice rising sheer from the ground, here glistening in naked, cracked, scooped-out rock; there dark with shaggy spruces (nearly the only foliage) — clutching the seams, tottering on the ledges, and stooping as if to tumble headlong from the narrow and sickening platforms. Up, up went the awful wall, stretching on, on, in a northerly direction for two miles, — a mile farther than the Indian Pass. Who would suppose, while viewing with astonished eye this famous pass, that here, lurking in its ambush, existed a gorge which

almost equaled the rocky wonder, — here, unknown
and unsuspected ! and he looked with utter amaze-
ment.   Almost equaled, I say, for the Pass secretes
a depth below the fallen rocks probably more than
one half the height above.

Although the term gorge is used, it is not strictly
one, scarcely as much so as the Pass; for
Mount McIntyre there slopes opposite the wall
throughout its length.   Here, Dix's Peak (the wall
is formed by the Dial) rounds down scarcely half
way the length of the wall at the southeast, leaving the balance of that side open, and thus letting
the eye out upon the vast sweep of woods below
and beyond, from which rises a mountain, the
Owl's Head, the most conspicuous object in sight.

Snow whitens the Gorge in large patches until
June, — patches that lie upon the open earth, —
while the Indian Pass only preserves its ice in its
deepest cavities.

While, as noted, the west branch of the Schroon
runs from the south portal of the Gorge, the northwest branch flows from southwest of the Dial, and,
like the first, empties into Mud Pond.

The Dial wall rises from one thousand to fifteen
hundred feet, equal to the apparent height of the
Pass.   A fringe of foliage trembles from the summit of the wall, and down the sheer descent as
much foliage as rock is discernible ; herein differing

from the Pass, which presents only a broken surface of bare gray rock, if the thinly scattered skeletons of white dead trees are excepted.

Fire had not swept the Gorge as at the Pass; the foliage was consequently fresh and green, and all as Nature had left it at its birth. And what fearful forge, I thought, as Elijah detailed his descriptions, had fashioned it! What sublime period saw it wrought in all its grandeur! No wonder Elijah's mind shrank appalled at the sight as it rose, rank above rank of trees, until the eye seemed as if it would never scale the summit.

The Gorge is narrow, only three or four rods in breadth, — the north end of Dix's Peak soaring loftily, as noticed, on the southeastern side. It is also blocked up with black spruces, so as to restrict materially the view. Still the magnificent battlement can be seen stretching along its two-mile extent, blackening all beneath with its majestic shadow.

The Gorge is unlike the Pass in another particular. While the wall of the latter shrinks, as it were, from contact, piling at its base a mass of débris (itself a mountain), that of the former allows your foot close to it and your hand to touch it. Neither does any waterfall bound from crevices of the wall. Nothing is visible but beetling crags, eyries of eagles, and tottering spruces, the haunt of ravens.

Through and through, from south to north, Elijah paced this mighty object of Nature. From its north end the ground falls as precipitously as it rises at its south. Here he let his eye rove over a mighty ocean of woods : at the left, toward old Indian Face, of the Lower Ausable ; on the right, in the direction of Split Rock, bordering the Elizabethtown road.

" What name do you give this gorge, Elijah? "

" Well," answered he, " it really has no name, but in speaking of it, I have always called it Mud Pond Gorge."

" Too much mud about that name, Elijah."

" I caught a wolf in a trap I had in the gorge last summer," said Elijah.

" That's it. The Wolf-Trap. Let that be the name, — The Wolf-Trap."

The jaws, or south portal, opened very much like one.

Elijah then ascended the Dial to kindle a bonfire on its globe.

His ascent was at the northeast, the only practicable place, where a stream dashed downward. It was four in the afternoon when he commenced his clamber, and he reached the foot of the rocky dome about six. He then began the ascent of this, the globe of the Atlas. After vast toil he achieved his task. The dilated sun was sink-

ing behind a peak of old Tahawus, that was red-
dened by the lustre. Beside the mountain rose
the Haystack, and between them and the Dial
surged the wild, wolf-jaw summits of the Ausable
Range, with the Boreas crests close at his left, and
at his right the Bald Peak of Moriah shining in
vermeil tints. The view at the east or opposite side
was different and very grand. He traced the South
Branch of the Boquet, flowing from the north opening of the Gorge, to its junction with the North
Branch, coming out of the mountains between the
Boquet and Keene valleys, and thence the river's
northeast path toward Lake Champlain, where it
empties. But the grandest sight was Dix's Peak.
Its enormous bulk rose so near, it seemed as if he
could toss a bullet against its side. It was smoothed
over with gold, as though a glittering yellow
mantle was cast over it. It rounded down to the
Gorge, north, four thousand feet, — rearing one
thousand feet higher a crest like the front of a lion ;
then falling gradually toward its southern termina-
tion to where it rose again in a sharpened peak like
the haunch of the same animal, until the vast mass
declined in a more easy slope to Macomb's Mountain at the south.

" The top of the ridge at the south rises as sharp
almost as a knife," continued Elijah. " It isn't
more than a foot wide, and slopes each side in a

rocky precipice covered with small spruces. It is **a**
quarter of a mile too."

" How did you pass over it, Elijah ? "

" As you ride a horse," answered Elijah. " It
wants a steady head to cross over it, for if you
should slip " —

" Well ? "

" You'd go to Davy's Locker to a certainty."

" What prospect is there from the top ? "

" Grand, but the same as from the Dial."

But to return to the kindling the fire on the top
of the Dial. He did so, and then descended as
rapidly as possible to see the effect.

A pyramid of fire flamed from the dome, flood-
ing it with crimson splendor, and touched the
Gorge in spots, speckling the bottom like huge fireflies. It must have been a strange spectacle that
weird pyramid. I thought, as Elijah paused in his
story, of the Parsee bending in devotion before his
kindled mountain-altar.

The afternoon of the next day saw my companions, myself, and the guides, at Elizabethtown.

Poke O'Moonshine stands on the Keeseville road,
midway the distance between Keeseville and the
" Valley." It is a mountain reared along the track
at its western side. Its aspect is wild and savage,
a miniature of the Indian Pass, and compared with
it, a pebble. Rocks from its breast have fallen at

its feet, and there is a cleft in the centre of the
mountain which affords a passage to its summit.

The first approach to it from Elizabethtown is
at the foot of a rough acclivity where stands a wild,
robber-looking red house upon the left, at the angle
of the road turning off to Clintonville. Trout Brook
courses at the left of this latter road. The acclivity
is broken and stony, and the forest begins to straggle
towards you. Thence the road roughens with one
glance of the gray crag in front until you arrive —
the woods breaking away, and open ground spread
ing before the rock — as an old woman said to me
— " to this dark, pokerish looking hole " of Poke
O'Moonshine, — which, indeed, is the meaning of
the odd, glimmering, picturesque name.

The finest view of the grim granite is, undoubtedly, in coming from Keeseville. You pass through
a vista of forest, and suddenly at a bend, the mountain stands full in front, blocking, to all appearance,
the road.

There is a younger brother of this rock on the
parallel Clintonville road. It stands, as this does,
at the track's west edge, and is a reduplication " in
small " of its kin. If this is " Poke O'Moonshine,"
that should be " Po' Shine." No cognomen is
attached to it, and in default of a better, why not
this its name.

Split Rock is another remarkable scene, eight

miles up the Boquet River, from Elizabethtown,
through the lovely scenery of New Russia, and four
miles from " Bishop's." It is a tremendous rocky
gorge breaking out of the woods, two or three hundred feet in length, through which the frenzied
river boils in a magnificent cataract, dashing down
the dark, wild ravine upon the right. There are
two or three falls near the main cataract. Two
miles above the gorge, the north and south branches
of the Boquet unite and pour their full maddened
volume through the foaming passage. The head
waters of the Schroon, or Hudson, at this point
flowing south and the Boquet running north, are
within thirty or forty rods of each other. What
curious intricacy of waters webbing almost their
feet together, and yet departing in two opposite
directions !

The " Walled Banks " of the Ausable River
present a wonderful scene, even in this region of
wonders. They commence two miles from Keeseville. This is a beautiful village of over three
thousand inhabitants, lying on both sides of the
Ausable River, its larger or northern portion being
in Clinton County, and its southern in Essex. It,
contains several churches, a Bank, and the Keeseville Academy; and is vividly alive with the iron
interest, owning some thirty mills and factories
devoted to this branch of industry.

The village consists of Main Street, crossing the Ausable by a bridge, and several lateral streets, with villas, cottages, and finely cultivated grounds in the suburbs. Thence extends a lovely region of hill-side and valley where the grain grows golden to the harvest, the grass steeps to the knee the stooping apple-trees, and where rural life is vocal around the frequent farm-house. There, likewise, are scattered woodlands with open floors of glade and dingle, while the manifold pasture fields are grouped with flock and herd. The charming Ausable Valley, holding her bright child in her lap, smiles southward toward her own cradle in the stern Adirondacks, whose peaks make the southern horizon grand. There dreams in delicate mist the far Tahawus; there glimmers the azure haze of the nearer Whiteface, while in the neighboring distance shines the clear blue mass of Moonshine.

From the above specified point of two miles, the Ausable River flows between walls of sandstone fifty feet in height; then glides placidly through low ground until it suddenly breaks into a cataract, and thence dashes wildly down a rocky channel to the village of Birmingham, where, at the " Chasm House," it bounds into a black abyss of sixty or seventy feet in depth and twenty in breadth. A bridge crosses the river at the cataract's head, and is continually enveloped in its mist. Here lives a rainbow, and this child of the sun smiles amid the mad turbulence like a seraph of love in the wrath and tumult of battle. Thence the wild waters dart along, now foaming through a frowning chasm, now down a rocky slope, a thunderbolt of flashing, roaring rapids, until the narrow walls expand into a circular form shaping a whirlpool.

Here in high water, the stream rises fifty feet, dashing, foaming, eddying with the back-water, but ordinarily presenting but a continuation of the rapids.

From the main stream, branches run at right angles through fissures, where the waters, checked in their fury, flow back with a gloss upon them like the sheen of ebony.

Down one of these fissures, at " High Bridge " (so called from a bridge once spanning a chasm, but now destroyed), hangs a perpendicular stairway of over two hundred steps.

Descending the stairs down, down, down, the foot rests at length on the narrow platform of rock which forms the jutting floor of the fissure. At either hand soar in the gloom to the height of a hundred feet the black, seamed, and stratified rocks, dripping in wetness, with deep angles, giving them an appearance of massive columns cracking under their own weight. High up glimmers a segment of sky with glimpses of dwarfed and drooping cedars.

Fancy might deem the rocks Titans, standing to the attack of Jove, and nearly smiting the heavens; though with sinews strained to bursting, their shaggy hair hanging, and their thunder-blackened forms bathed in the moisture of their toil.

Below, voiceless and in ebony, flows the stream through the spectral dusk, like Styx seen by ghostly light.

On dashes and plunges the main stream until, emerging from the chasm, it pursues its gladdened course through fields and meadows to Lake Champlain.

The rocky path of this catapult of water is two miles, the walls (of the Potsdam sandstone) attaining a vertical height of from seventy-five to one hundred and fifty feet, with a breadth of from eight feet to thirty.

How like the stream to the human heart falling into calamity and battling with its narrow fortunes; now whirling in frenzy, now retiring into dark and sullen exclusion, until by a change of fate it is freed from its fetters, and smiles along in its broad and prosperous pathway to the end.

Three days after my return from the Gorge, I left Elizabethtown in a private conveyance for Scott's, taking the famous Keene Pass, or Edmunds' Ponds, in my route. Where the road to the Pass left the highway near the village of Keene, again the billowy

13

pile of mountains, tumbling splendidly upon the valley, met my admiring gaze.

The road now roughened rapidly, and we began winding up an ascent. Woods closed around us, interspersed with rough clearings.

And thus in life. It is by the rough, ascending road that we attain our objects.

"Sweet are the uses of adversity."

There is a tree in Sumatra that puts forth its leaves and flowers, fraught with the richest fragrance, only in the night. Day sees it robbed of its breath, and stripped of its blossoms and its gréen. So the darkness of adverse fate draws the brightest and sweetest virtues from the same soul that in the sunshine of prosperity shows but a scentless barrenness of good.

At length the road ran entirely through these clearings, until we reached the Pass, which we did at mid-day. It was a narrow cleft, with tall parallel mountains either side. The two ponds lay black and glossy, filling entirely the crevice. Formerly there was only one pond, but an enormous slide down the centre of the southeastern mountain divided it by a broad bridge of earth, which is now coursed by a small stream uniting the two sheets. The scene was as wild and savage as any in the wild and savage Adirondacks. Opposite glared the ragged

broken slide, striping its mountain — one of the
Keene Range — with a torrent tumbling into the
pond at its foot, with Big Pitch-Off Mountain
frowning steeply on the other, or northwestern side.
Iron ore unburied by the slide crops out from the
awful gash of the mountain's flank, showing how
prevalent is the ore throughout the whole region.
The road ran to the north of the ponds by means
of a narrow and dangerous causeway — a corduroy
— so narrow that the hubs of the wheels almost
impended over the water all the mile's distance
through the Pass. At the west end the mountains
sank into a hollow similar to the crescents at Lakes
Colden and Avalanche.

We were glad when we shook off the shadows
of this sublime but gloomy Pass, and launched once
more on our road, which still lay through the forest,
with here and there a wild field. The "South
Meadows" (Wild Meadows) of Scott begin a few
miles at the south, and embrace about a thousand
acres. At a point directly north of the eastern slope
of Mount Colden, three streams — one on the southeast, another at the northeast, and the third flowing
from the direction of Colden — meet, and form the
south branch of the West Ausable. This branch runs
westerly, until it receives a large stream from the
direction of Lake Avalanche; then it bends northerly, where the main stream of the West Ausable,

flowing from the Indian Pass, receives it, and running thence north, receives also Chubb River from Lake Placid, opposite Thompson's Meadows.

The South Meadows are shaped like an old fashioned pair of bellows, the broad end lying toward the east, and the narrow end to the west, the mountains shutting in the spout of the bellows, and forming a grand, wild gorge.

The Meadows are apparently quite flat, but are, in reality, full of hollows, rendering the walking very uncomfortable through the sword-grass, tickle-grass, blue-joint and rattlesnake grass, with which the meadows are covered; while on either side slope hills dense with bushes of the huckleberry.

The four miles were soon traversed from the ponds to where we regained the highway, or mountain-road, and, after a brief distance, I hailed with pleasure the white domicile of Robert G. Scott, standing in its rural plateau ; with its " Cobble " or East bluff — its smooth northern meadows — its Indian Pass Portal at the south, over the unbroken sea of woods — with Old Wallface stretching a grand, green battlement within its two-mile distance, and the sublime mountain-tops turreting the horizon's sweep: one magnificent and mighty circle.

In the night, the sky from its gold-dotted purple blackened to a magnificent thunder-storm.   Glare after glare, and roll upon roll, shone and sounded.

I gazed at the flaming bursts and hearkened to the fearful crashes, with the mountain and forest landscape gleaming and vanishing as if the heavens were one grand red eye winking the black scene fitfully into sight. As I looked and listened, the flashing and roaring peaks piling the horizon became audible to my inner sense, and my ear was filled with their sublime voices.

" Slaves ! " thundered Tahawus, glaring in wrathful crimson. " Are ye frightened that ye start so ? Methought, at the last flash of the storm's eye ye would bound from your rocky skins ! "

" Slaves ! " shouted McIntyre. " This to me, a king, lifting a crest scarcely lower than thine own, and bearing a chasm [1] in my heart that almost equals thy grand Panther Gorge ! aye, quite, for puny Haystack aids in forming thine, O stern Tahawus ! "

" Slaves ! " roared Colden. " I, the Wild-Cat of the Adirondacks ! — I, frighted by the thunder and lightning of the storm, hurling as I do from peak to base thunders and lightnings of my own, and thus even rivaling thee, Tahawus ! I am slave to none, and frightened at naught ! " and he seemed to lift his shoulder in disdain while his stately tones echoed and reëchoed.

---

[1] There is a gorge in this mountain cloven from a point midway its summit down to its base.

" Slaves ! " pealed Mount Seward.   " I, monarch of a family of kings ! [1]   How darest thou, Tahawus ! Thou, too, wert startled at the flash !   I saw thee ! " and the mountain's eye shone fiercely.

" Slaves ! " crashed Whiteface.   " This to one that only stoops to thee, Tahawus ! one who looks down from his cloudy pinnacle upon a gorge and cataract, thou, King of the Adirondacks, canst not equal !   Thy Panther Gorge !   Why, its length compares not even with my slide, while by miles alone my gorge is measured !   Thy Opalescent ! What, that paltry ribbon of white to the two wild torrents flashing with their wrath down my steep, towering sides !   And the speck of a brooklet that creeps frightened nearly from its life along thy gloomy gorge !   The savage Ausable flows black through mine, and plunges down a precipice with strength that would dash a struggling eagle to his death and tear thy stateliest pine-tree into atoms ! I " —

" Silence ! "   Tahawus thundered breaking in upon a harangue that threatened to be interminable. " Why do ye not, like Santanoni, Henderson, and Wallface, the Dial and stern, dark Gothics, to say nothing of my lesser vassals, hold your tongues when your monarch speaks ?   Listen to " —

---

[1] **Mount Seward**, as before observed, is formed by a cluster of peaks.

" Hold ! " shouted Wallface. " I have tried to speak ever since thou didst first break out ! I scorn the name of slave as deeply as the rest ! I, holding to the storm a breastplate on which, since first the Creator formed me, a million storms have dashed in vain, and against which centuries have crumbled, and will crumble ! I wonder at thee, King ! "

" And I," the Dial sounded, — " I with a front of mail second only to the breastplate of Wallface, — I among thy slaves, Tahawus ! I hurl thy taunt from me in disdain, O Piercer of the Cloud ! " and he seemed to raise higher his head in the wild crimson of his anger.

As for Dix's Peak, he, being monarch of his own mountains, which do not belong to the tribe of the Adirondacks, and consequently not putting the cap of the Cloud Piercer on his head, didn't say anything.

But again the Dial spoke : " My gorge below hath also heard thy taunt, and doth scorn like me thy " —

" Silence ! " once more Tahawus thundered. " But first in answer to Seward, The Mountain of the Eye. I did start, but it was in wrath, for a spark of the storm's fire kindled a fibre of a pine at the base of my forehead, and it stung me. But know,"—and a now lambent flame played round his head, while his deepened accents kindlier sounded, — " know that your King spoke thus to rouse ye, that ye might hearken farther to his words. And this, my children ! Let self-reliance be the rock of your natures ! — self-reliance wrought of the loftiest attributes : courage that conquers all storms, even the storm of dissolution ; faith which feels that the chastening God is the loving Father ; patience that restrains and endures with divine belief of good to come ; energy that fills the soul with live propulsion, and hope, sister-star of faith and patience, that shines serenely on the present, and streams brightly into the future. No matter then the fiercest tempest, for ye are invincible in the strength of courage, the assurance of faith, the restraint of patience, the propulsion of energy, and the happiness of hope."

The voice ceased, and I looked out. The storm had passed away, the sky was beaming with its stars, but I felt a whisper through the heavenly quiet. " Heed, O heart, the lesson of the mountain ! Whatever lot may happen, whatever woe betide, be self-reliance thine, in the courage that dares, in the faith that assures, in the patience that waits, in the energy that impels, and the hope that makes happy. So shalt thou keep thyself firm in the strength of peace. So shalt thou lift thy brow into the serene sunshine, with the vanquished clouds cowering at thy feet. So shalt thou look the world straight in its cruel eye, until that eye quails beneath thy steady gaze, and the hand that would have grasped thy throat strews flowers in thy pathway. Victor in life instead of victim, thou shalt thus break down every barrier, bear down every foe, and chain success a lasting captive at thy car of triumph.

END.

ADIRONDACK CLASSICS

Purple Mountain Press and Harbor Hill Books

A History of the Adirondacks
by Alfred L. Donaldson

Donaldson's *History* is recognized as the major work about the entire region and, as such, has remained unsurpassed since its first publication in 1921. This is an unabridged reprint with a biographical sketch by John Duquette. 766 pages in two volumes, illustrated, cloth.

Long Lake
by John Todd

This is a facsimile of the earliest book entirely devoted to an Adirondack topic. A new introduction by Warder H. Cadbury presents the fascinating story of the Adirondacks in the 1840s. The cover duplicates the original 1845 binding.
128 pages, cloth.

The Birch Bark Books of Henry Abbott
**Sporting Adventures and Nature Observations
in the Adirondacks in the early 1900s**

Henry Abbott spent summers at Long Lake. These are his stories of beavers and bears, of rivers and ponds and summits. Originally printed in editions of fewer than 100 copies (1914–1932), this rare collection is reprinted in one volume for the first time. Introduction by Vincent Engels.
288 pages, 163 illustrations and maps, cloth.

Through the Adirondacks in Eighteen Days
by Martin V. B. Ives

This is a reprint of a scarce 1899 edition which describes a "fact-finding" trip made by a New York State legislative committee to study the Adirondacks to determing what lands should be added to the forest preserve. New introduction by Neal S. Burdick.
128 pages, 57 illustrations, map, cloth.

Historical Sketches of Northern New York and the Adirondack Wilderness
by Nathaniel B. Sylvester
The first comprehensive history of the Adirondacks, recognized as the only logical predecessor of Donaldson's *History*. Reprint of the 1877 edition.
316 pages, paperback.

Castorland
French Refugees in the Western Adirondacks, 1793-1814
by Edith Pilcher
This new study of the early French settlers in the Black River Valley, based on recently discovered documents, is supported by a wealth of carefully selected illustrations, facsimiles and maps.
254 pages, 52 illustrations and maps, cloth.

The French Occupation of the Champlain Valley
by Guy Omeron Coolidge
One of the most important sources for information about the French in the Northeast, this is the first complete edition in book form of articles appearing in periodicals 1938–1940. A biographical index has been added.
224 pages, illustrated, cloth.

History of Lake Champlain, 1609–1814
by Peter S. Palmer
Within 65 years three major wars were fought on the shores and waters of Lake Champlain. Palmer (1814-1890) chronicles the early history of the lake so well that this book has been a resource for over 100 years.
250 pages, illustrated, paperback.

Sails and Steam in the Mountains
A Maritime and Military History of Lake George and Lake Champlain
by Russell P. Bellico
This is the first comprehensive history of the two lakes in 30 years. The use of original diaries and journals adds an exciting first-hand dimension to the narrative that follows the history of the two lakes from the French and Indian War through the canal and steamboat eras and includes all of the recent, exciting underwater archaeological discoveries.
400 pages, over 100 illustrations, large format, cloth and paperback.

Wildlife and Wilderness
A History of Adirondack Mammals
by Philip G. Terrie

A thorough cultural history of man's interaction with fur-bearing and game animals of the North Country, this book examines the extirpation of the moose, elk, panther, and beaver and the politics, ethics, and ecology that play a part in attempts to reintroduce some of the large mammals to their former ranges.

176 pages, illustrated, paperback.

North Country Almanac
Journal of the Adirondack Seasons
by Robert F. Hall

The changing seasons are followed in a series of essays inspired by the plants, animals and birds of the North Country by the former *Conservationist* editor.

136 pages, paperback.

On the Adirondack Survey With Verplanck Colvin
The Diaries of Percy Reese Morgan
edited by Norman Van Valkenburgh

Percy Reese Morgan (1878-1961) was a college student when he joined the crew of Verplanck Colvin's famed Adirondack Survey. His diaries provide a candid look at camp life during the summers of 1895 and 1896.

96 pages, illustrated, paperback.

The High Peaks of Essex
The Adirondack Mountains of Orson Schofield Phelps
edited by Bill Healy

Bill Healy recounts the adventure of discovering a long-known but lost manuscript by Adirondack guide "Old Mountain" Phelps (1817–1905). This is the earliest writing about the mountains by a person who lived there.

114 pages, illustrated, paperback.

Pages from Adirondack History
by Robert Hall

A collection of Rob Hall's best observations on the people, places, and events that shaped the story of the North Country.

152 pages, paperback.

Alfred Billings Street
1811-1881

ALFRED BILLINGS STREET was an attorney who practiced in Monticello, New York until 1839 when he moved to Albany. There he devoted his life to literature and poetry and later became director of the New York State Library (1842–1862 — he remained law librarian until 1868). His best known works are his historical poems "The Burning of Schenectady" (1842) and "Frontenac" (1849) and a prose work, *Woods and Waters; or, The Saranacs and Racket* (1860).

•

THE ILLUSTRATION used on the front and back covers is taken from the chapter "The Adirondack Region" in William Cullen Bryant's *Picturesque America*, vol. 2, 1874. It is a wood engraving of the Indian Pass after a drawing by Harry Fenn and is reproduced through the courtesy of With Pipe and Book, Lake Placid, New York.

•

PURPLE MOUNTAIN PRESS, LTD. is a publishing company committed to producing the best original books of regional interest as well as bringing back into print significant older works. It also publishes under the Harbor Hill imprint. For a free catalog of over 300 hard-to-find books about the Adirondacks and New York State, write: Purple Mountain Press, Ltd., P.O. Box E3, Fleischmanns, NY 12430, call: 914-254-4062, or fax: 914-254-4476.